TWILIGHT OVER THE TEMPLES:

The Close of Cambodia's Belle Epoque

Leslie Fielding read History at Cambridge, where he is an Honorary Fellow of Emmanuel College, and Persian at the School of Oriental and African Studies, London. He joined the then Foreign Service in 1956, working initially in Tehran and (briefly) Singapore, before being put in charge of the British Embassy in Phnom Penh, Cambodia, 1964-1966. His subsequent diplomatic career took him to Paris, in the political section; Brussels, as a Director in the European Commission; Tokyo, as EU Ambassador; and back to Brussels, as Director-General for External Relations. He has been a Visiting Fellow at St Antony's College, Oxford, and Vice-Chancellor of the University of Sussex. His autobiography, *Kindly Call Me God*, was published in 2009 and his *Before the Killing Fields: Witness to Cambodia and the Vietnam War*, in 2008. Previously, he had contributed to two travel anthologies: *Travellers' Tales*, in 1999 and *More Travellers' Tales*, in 2005. He is married to the medievalist, Sally Harvey; they have two children, and live in Shropshire. Sir Leslie was knighted in 1988.

Twilight Over The Temples:

The Close of Cambodia's Belle Epoque

I am not he. You are not she. These are not those. All characters in this screen play, other than those clearly in the public domain, are wholly or largely fictitious. Events and their locations are a mixture of the real and the imaginary. The sequence of real-life international developments affecting Indo-China between 1963 and 1970 has been accelerated and compressed, for dramatic purposes.

[handwritten dedication and signature]

Leslie Fielding

Boermans Books

The right of Leslie Fielding to be identified as the author of this work has been asserted by him in accordance with the Copyright, Designs and Patent Act 1988.

All rights reserved. Except for brief quotations in a review, this book, or any part thereof, may not be reproduced, stored in or introduced into a retrieval system, or transmitted in any form or by any means, electronic, mechanical, photocopying, recording or otherwise, without the prior written permission of the publishers.

ISBN 978-0-9562167-2-4

A full CIP record for this book is available from the British Library.
A Full CIP record is available from the Library of Congress
Library of Congress Catalog Card Number: available
Front cover: Image of a ruined temple at Angkor Wat, from an oil painting by Tes-Phār, 1966. Author's own collection.
Back cover: Angkor Wat.
               Cambodian Dancer reproduced with kind permission of Denise Heywood from her book "Cambodian Dancers: Celebration of the Gods" (2008).
Page iii: Photograph of the author.
Photographs on pp23/24: The British Embassy Chancery, Phnom Penh, after attack by rioters on 11 March 1964.
Published in 2011 by Boermans Books.
Printed in Times New Roman 10 pt.
Printed and bound in Great Britain by York Publishing Services.

Acknowledgements

I am grateful to Peter Burden, for pointing the way;
and to Brian Patrick Shiel, for guiding my faltering footsteps.

Dedication

To John Shakespeare
Head of Chancery, Phnom Penh,
and his British Embassy and British Council
colleagues,
for their coolness and courage,
11 March 1964.

(a hard act to follow!)

Contents

Acknowledgements	vii
Dedication	ix
Foreword	xiii
Author's Introduction	xv
Principal Protagonists, in order of appearance	1
Introduction: From Fort William to Washington	3
Part One: Good Morning, Cambodia!	9
Part Two: High Noon	59
Part Three: Bolt from a Blue Sky	73
Part Four: The Fading of the Light	89
The Ending: Forty Years On	109
Background Reading	117
Historical Note: Sirik Matak's Last Stand	121
Also by Leslie Fielding	123

Foreword

Leslie Fielding's screenplay about a young diplomat in Cambodia is fiction and drama, not autobiography or conventional documentary. The author offers adventure, intrigue, action and romance, thrills and spills, with a compelling cast of characters. Also, an ironic ending.

Sadly, however, he writes in the context of a real-time international peace negotiation, the failure of which had ultimately appalling consequences for a peaceful people and a nation which deserved better. For, "Twilight over the Temples" has a factual basis – the history of Cambodia in the '60s and early '70s, leading up to the Killing Fields. Entertainment apart, the narrative inevitably invites political reflection.

A first reaction has to be to acknowledge the calibre and resource of Britain's Diplomatic Service – and, when required, even the courage of its operatives in the field. (The Dedication alludes to the mob attack on the British Embassy in Phnom Penh in March 1964). A diplomat, when distant from his or her home base, can lead a life far removed from the champagne and caviar image of popular misconception.

This loyal, professional Service, never entirely a favourite with Margaret Thatcher, was – with disastrous consequences – marginalized and muzzled under Tony Blair, who did not welcome truth spoken to power, nor expert advice at variance from that of his (mostly inexpert) personal advisors. Happily, under the new coalition government, this is now being corrected. For a medium-sized power, facing serious problems in a darkening international landscape, the lesson for Britain is clear, irrespective of party politics.

Then, there is the matter of Britain's alliance with the United States. Everyone agrees that this is an absolutely vital partnership. But it has to rest on a firm foundation of mutual frankness and trust, in which the junior partner is ready to speak out, as well as put his money where his mouth is, when required. In Indo-China, Harold Wilson was right to resist repeated US pressure to commit British troops to the unwise and unwinnable war in Vietnam; and to concentrate instead, as Sir Anthony Eden had done at the time of the French defeat and withdrawal in the mid 1950s, on the search for a realistic settlement through negotiation.

The basic diplomatic dilemma facing Cambodia in the '60s is well described in the Command Paper of June 1965 cited at the end of the Background Reading. The tragedy lay in British inability to convince President Johnson to go for a neutralised Cambodia, before it was too late. If Kennedy had lived, and Macmillan not fallen sick, it might have been different. *Hinc illae lacrimae!*

But now, do please fasten your safety belts and read on – keeping pocket handkerchiefs handy, for the conclusion.

Author's Introduction

This is a story about conflict between East and West. The heart of the story lies in the tragic love which unites an Eastern woman and a Western man – and the cultural conflict which it brings to the surface. This, in the context of high international tension, leading to war and eventually even genocide.

A young diplomat pursues honour and glory in an exotic and distant land. He takes on the world, charms a king and falls in love. But the fairytale fades. His duties draw him deep into the turbulent world of plot and counterplot in pre-revolutionary Cambodia. Betrayal comes from an unexpected quarter and paves the way to personal tragedy and national disaster.

The action mostly takes place in exotic settings in Cambodia in the 1960s. The characters are unwitting puppets in the hands of the White House and the People's Palace in Beijing. Messianic, but ill-judged and badly informed, decisions by President Johnson have the unintended consequence of opening the way to total destabilisation. Eventually, to the murder of possibly approaching a quarter of the civilian population of Cambodia by a monster – the revolutionary Marxist, Pol Pot – aided and abetted by that other Communist monster, Chairman Mao Tse-tung.

On the ground, decent people struggle to make the best of a bad situation.

Principal Protagonists, in order of appearance

Robert Campbell	Youthful British Chargé d'Affaires in Phnom Penh.
Noel Rankin	Experienced, elderly Australian ambassador.
Martine Lefè vre	Stunningly beautiful daughter of a Cambodian Princess and a French General.
Prince Monivong Kantol	Prime Minister
General Lefè vre	Head of the French Military Mission and father of Martine.
General Lon Nol	Right-wing army chief, who eventually deposes the King.
Maurice LeBrun	Left-wing French advisor to the King, eventually murdered
Dan McGuire	CIA chief, eventually expelled.
The King	Intelligent and sympathetic, but ultimately doomed, Deva-Raja (God King).
Saloth Sar	Later known as Pol Pot.

TWILIGHT OVER THE TEMPLES

INTRODUCTION: FROM FORT WILLIAM TO WASHINGTON

Int. A castle in the Scottish Highlands. Spring 2012. Night time.

An oak-panelled bedroom, dimly lit. In the four-poster bed, two figures, an elderly Scotsman and his American wife. LORD *and* LADY CAMPBELL. *The man is twitching and turning. Something in his deep subconscious is tormenting him. He groans and mutters in his sleep; then comes to, with a start. The woman is lying still, but wide awake.*

LORD CAMPBELL: No. *NO!* ...... Where *am* I? God! That was awful.

LADY CAMPBELL: Darling, not Cambodia *again?* Like last night? And every night this week?

LORD CAMPBELL: Y-Yes it was! (*Still shaking a little*). Now that we know what happened – about the genocide – I'm getting the same nightmare, night after night. Walking through a deserted city. Phnom Penh. No one about. Just wrecked cars on the street; broken doors and windows in the buildings. And the crunch – of human bones under my feet.

LADY CAMPBELL: Robert Campbell, this *cannot* continue. You're still trembling. We've really got to talk. I can't help *you*, unless you open up to *me*. Typical 'Brit' – all 'stiff upper lip' and 'bite the bullet'! But it won't do. You've got to let it all hang out. Starting *now*. This minute!

LORD CAMPBELL: It all began, in the 'sixties, in Washington. Before I met you. I was new to the Washington scene, a junior in the Embassy. But feet under the table. Plenty to do. That I liked doing. One evening, a reception at the White House....

Int. The White House, Washington. Late spring in the 'sixties. An evening reception.

MR ROBERT CAMPBELL, *a young high-flyer at the British Embassy, is moving around the salons, seeking out his acquaintances and contacts among staffers from the West Wing and the Hill; senior people at State; 'Oped' writers from the Washington Post/the New York Times. A civilised setting. But also the palpable sense of power being brokered, major international business being transacted.* CAMPBELL *seems in his element. His Ambassador has just arrived, to make a brief 'acte de presence'.* CAMPBELL *(following Embassy protocol) moves across to pay his respects, see whether his chief needs rescuing from a bore, needs his glass replenishing. Whatever.*

BRITISH AMBASSADOR IN WASHINGTON: Ah, Robert! Just the man. A word in your ear, if I may? Before I move on. I need to see you in my office. First thing tomorrow, please.

ROBERT CAMPBELL: Sir?

4

BRITISH AMBASSADOR: The FO want to pass you a poisoned chalice. Can't go into it now. Sorry – must dash!

ROBERT CAMPBELL: Yes, Sir. Good night.

Int. The British Embassy, Washington. The following morning.

A secretary's office, with large windows looking down onto Massachusetts Avenue. The traffic passes silently, unheard through the triple glazing. A side door opens, to admit ROBERT CAMPBELL, *indignant, who has just returned from seeing the Ambassador. The* SECRETARY *looks up from behind her typewriter, surprised - and slightly alarmed.*

SECRETARY: Bob? What happened with the Ambassador? You look upset!

ROBERT CAMPBELL: You bet I'm upset. You'd never guess. London want me out of here and into Cambodia. At once, if not before. Believe it! In ten day's time, to be precise.

SECRETARY: Why? What *have* you done? We love you. We want you *here*!

A MALE COLLEAGUE OF CAMPBELL: (*entering from the door on the other side – he and Campbell share the same secretary*) Bob, what's all this about? You've only been with us in Washington since September.

ROBERT CAMPBELL: You've seen the international TV coverage, out there. Mobs roaming the streets. Place apparently becoming a 'Failed State'. That sort of thing.

COLLEAGUE: Yes. But, so what? What's it got to do with *you*?

ROBERT CAMPBELL: H.E. says that the FO have just decided to pull out all the Embassy married staff, with their families and dependants. In fact, pretty well every one there. The Ambassador included. The whole lot to be replaced by a new skeleton staff. To be led by me.

COLLEAGUE: But why pick on Bob Campbell to fill the gap, for Pete's sake?

ROBERT CAMPBELL: I'm single and expendable. They need a fluent French speaker. Someone good at Judo. H.E. says he's done his best. Genuinely sorry to be losing me and all that. But London simply won't budge.

COLLEAGUE: So where's the sweetener? What's in it for *you?*

ROBERT CAMPBELL: A modest promotion. And I get to be Head of Mission – Chargé d'Affaires in Cambodia. Indefinitely and without relief, maybe for long years ahead. Until I die of boredom, old age, or enemy action.

COLLEAGUE: Flippin' heck! Remember the memoirs of Sir Winston Churchill's medical advisor? Didn't the old boy say something like (*imitates Churchill's drawl*) "I didn't become Her Majesty's First Minister of State, to bother about bloody places like Cambodia!"?

ROBERT CAMPBELL: Yeah!

COLLEAGUE: Frankly Bob – you always were an ambitious toad. You deserve your come-uppance.

(*Exits, grinning.* CAMPBELL *snatches up a pencil and hurls it after him*).

ROBERT CAMPBELL: Bastard. Out!

SECRETARY: Bob: take me with you! To Cambodia!

ROBERT CAMPBELL: (*shakes his head*) Nope! Too dangerous. Even *your* skills at close combat would not be up to it!

SECRETARY: Then take me out to the Hay Adams, for dinner tonight.

ROBERT CAMPBELL: Yep! Why not? (*Pauses, looking out of the window over Washington*). I am going to miss Washington. (*Turns back from the window, guiltily and in haste*). Oh yes, and miss you too, of course, Louise. (*Exits, pursued by a second pencil*).

SECRETARY: Bastard. Out!

PART ONE: GOOD MORNING, CAMBODIA!

Ext. Phnom Penh International Airport. Ten days later.

Part super-modern building, part tin shack. Brilliant blue subtropical sky and burning noonday sun. The heat and humidity radiate from the tarmac, imparting a slight ripple effect to the buildings and control tower. CAMPBELL *walks away from the Air Singapore Boeing 707, towards Customs and Immigration. A young, cool-looking English girl,* JUNE DAWSON, *greets him.*

JUNE DAWSON: Robert Campbell? Nice flight?
ROBERT CAMPBELL: That's me. Yes thanks. And who are *you?*
JUNE DAWSON: I am the Ambassador's PA, June Dawson. I have been sent to meet you – all the men are tied up, at the moment.

They shake hands. CAMPBELL *grins, but* JUNE *is tense and unsmiling.*

ROBERT CAMPBELL: Glad to meet you. Thanks for coming out here. I really could have managed by taxi or something.
JUNE DAWSON: Afraid Phnom Penh isn't like that. You need someone with this diplomatic *laissez-passer*, to get you safely through and into town. Especially today.
ROBERT CAMPBELL: Anything wrong?
JUNE DAWSON: We are expecting another demonstration, bigger than usual, outside our Embassy. Also, the American, I believe.
ROBERT CAMPBELL: Gosh. Golly gumdrops. Let's get going.

They approach surly immigration officers. CAMPBELL *presents his passport. They take their time looking at it, turning every page, critically. In baggage reclaim, Customs officers demand that* CAMPBELL *open his two suitcases and his carry-on bag.* CAMPBELL *hesitates.* JUNE *waves her 'laissez-passer'. Reluctantly, the Customs let them through. Outside on the pavement, standing beside a highly polished, black Embassy station wagon, the Cambodian driver smiles and gives a half bow – the first friendly face so far.* CAMPBELL *introduces himself, democratically. They shake hands. The driver is called Hong.*

> JUNE DAWSON: You'll be staying with H.E. at the Residence, for the first few days. But we'd better head direct to the Chancery right now – dear Hong here will take your luggage on to the Residence. We're expecting serious trouble. But *serious.*

Ext. The main boulevards of the city.

Surging crowds on the pavements, but the streets themselves ominously empty of normal traffic. Loudspeakers relay shouted slogans and high-pitched, hysterical speeches. The station wagon drives past processions forming up. Placards are being distributed by uniformed police.

> ROBERT CAMPBELL: (*turning to* JUNE DAWSON, *after a careful look at the demonstrators*) They seem to be mostly anti-American. "Yankee go home", sort of stuff.
>
> JUNE DAWSON: They don't often distinguish between us and the Americans. We both tend to get lumped together as the

common enemy. Look (*points to one banner*): "Perfidious Albion". That means us.

They get nearer the British Embassy Chancery building, on Independence Avenue, a broad boulevard, leading up to an arch in red sandstone commemorating the grant of Independence to Cambodia by France in 1953. Three or four rows of demonstrators are lined up on the opposite side of the street, chanting and shouting slogans. DAWSON *averts her gaze; but* CAMPBELL *stares at them, incredulously.*

Ext. The Chancery compound, surrounded by an eight foot wall.

From a flagpole in the middle of a lawn, a large Union Jack is flying. The office building is French Colonial in style – airy and elegant, white washed walls under a red tile roof. In the noonday sun, the Chancery looks cool and inviting, ground floor windows open, to show overhead ceiling fans turning. On the first floor, the office windows are closed and air conditioning units are whirring. The station wagon enters through wrought iron gates and draws up to a porch covering the main entrance. CAMPBELL *and* DAWSON *disembark. The vehicle exits the compound briskly.* HONG THE DRIVER *ducking his head apprehensively, as he passes by the demonstrators. An Englishman in white shorts and short-sleeved shirt emerges to greet the arrivals. He is the* VICE-CONSUL.

VICE-CONSUL: Robert Campbell? Am I pleased to see *you!* We've got big problems. I'm Rob Smith, by the way – the Vice-

Consul. Come inside.

The group enter. JUNE *disappears upstairs, to the confidential offices. The two men sit down in the Vice-Consul's high ceilinged ground floor office.*

VICE-CONSUL: We're really short-handed at the moment. The Military Attaché got flown out sick, last month. Successor not here, yet. The Second Secretary is up-country, visiting a rubber plantation. The Consul has just popped over to Bangkok, carrying the Diplomatic Bag. Otherwise, the girls and boys are all here to man the fort: clerks, secretaries, diplomatic wireless operator.

ROBERT CAMPBELL: And the Ambassador? I haven't met him yet.

VICE-CONSUL: Went over to the US Embassy, to see his opposite number. But now he's trapped. The Yanks are absolutely hemmed in by demonstrators. In fact, under mob attack. So you're in charge of us all, till H.E. gets back.

ROBERT CAMPBELL: Great! Nothing like jumping in the deep end. What do you expect to happen?

VICE-CONSUL: Not sure. On past form, just a march past and some shouting. Maybe a petition of protest handed in at the main gate. A few rocks. But, this time, we've heard on the grapevine that it could get worse. So our local Cambodian staff have been sent home – they're more likely to be lynched by the mob than we are. And we've moved all the official transport out, too. (*Pointing through the open window to half a dozen saloon cars, parked in the shade, at the edge of the compound*).

Leaving just the private cars of the UK staff.

ROBERT CAMPBELL: OK. What do you suggest we do next?

VICE-CONSUL: Stand outside with me, by the gateway onto the street. Look unconcerned. Shake hands with the two Cambodian policemen on duty. Be ready to receive any petitions. Come back inside, if they start throwing things.

ROBERT CAMPBELL: Let's do it. But perhaps I'd better say hello to the staff, first? And take a quick look round, upstairs?

They leave the Vice-Consul's office. CAMPBELL *looks into the various offices and introduces himself briefly to the clerical and secretarial staff. He shakes hands all round. Then goes back outside, with the* VICE-CONSUL. *They cross the lawn and stand in the gateway.*

Ext. The street outside the Embassy.

The crowd is now about a thousand strong. A brass band has arrived and starts to play martial music. CAMPBELL *and the* VICE-CONSUL *are waved back into the Embassy building by the police, who then close the wrought iron gates. A loudspeaker van draws up. A man climbs on the roof and harangues the crowd, who reach new heights of excitement. They begin chanting frenetically, in unison.* CAMPBELL *emerges onto the first floor balcony to watch. Suddenly, the sky is darkened by hundreds of stones hurled from the front ranks of the crowd. These shatter windows, rattle the shutters and fall against the walls, with the noise of heavy hail.* CAMPBELL *dodges back inside. The staff close and bolt all doors.*

The crowd swarm over the wall, into the compound.

Int. Inside the Chancery.

CAMPBELL *supervises the evacuation of the ground floor, as the mob starts to break in. Everyone retreats to the so-called 'security zone' on the first floor, behind an open metal grill covering the foot of the staircase, and a second such grill at the top of the staircase, protecting a windowless corridor in which the staff take cover – the first floor offices on either side are full of flying glass.*

Ext. The Chancery Compound.

Looting in progress. The crowd is throwing out chairs, telephones, stationery, consular records, reference books, etc. Rioters hammer the parked cars with rocks, dragging two or three towards the flagpole, where they build a bonfire; but are stopped by the police from setting light to it and the vehicles. Police reinforcements arrive and persuade the mob to leave the compound and return to the street. The loudspeaker van falls silent.

CAMPBELL *goes out into the open and starts talking in French to three authoritative-looking, well-dressed mob leaders, evidently government officials, just inside the gates. He explains that there are some frightened young girls inside, whom the police must escort to their homes. He is, however, once more pushed back inside the building, followed by a few stones, which miss him. The crowd in the street grows even larger; the loudspeaker van resumes its cacophony. With a roar, the mob once more surges forward, brushing the police aside.*

Int. Inside.

The rioters flood into the Chancery building and start hammering against the downstairs grill. This gives way. Mob leaders ascend the staircase, tearing down pictures as they go.

CAMPBELL emerges from the dark corridor on the first floor, the remaining refuge of the Embassy staff. He stands at the top of the staircase. Confronts a man who seems to be the riot leader. The leader attempts to push past CAMPBELL. CAMPBELL *brings him down, effortlessly, with a Judo throw. Another rioter steps up, and* CAMPBELL *throws him, also – but with greater violence. The remaining rioters hold back, undecided.*

ROBERT CAMPBELL: (*speaking forcefully, in French: subtitles as follows*) Sorry, but you are stopping, right there. No further forward, if you please. Things have gone quite far enough. The police require you all to leave the building, immediately.

That moment, three policemen arrive in the hall below. Seeing them, the leader picks himself up, shrugs his shoulders and starts to lead his colleagues down the stairs. CAMPBELL *follows them.*

Ext. Outside.

Now plenty of police, shepherding the rioters out of the Chancery building, across the compound, and back out onto the street. Anti-riot vans arrive, disgorging tough looking paramilitaries, in steel helmets. Things calm down.

A middle-aged Englishman slips into the compound by a side gate. *He is wearing a fawn-coloured, lightweight suit, soiled by the rotten vegetables with which he has been pelted, one sleeve slightly singed by a petrol bomb. He is* SIR BERTRAM BUDELY, *the British Ambassador, who has managed to walk back unnoticed from the American Embassy, half a mile away.*

Int. The wrecked ground floor of the Chancery building, where ROBERT CAMPBELL **is inspecting the damage.**

The Ambassador enters.

SIR BERTRAM: (*collected, and determined to show himself in a good light*) Robert Campbell, I presume? Bertram Budely, your Ambassador. Welcome to Cambodia!

ROBERT CAMPBELL: (*respectful, but dishevelled and in a state of controlled shock*) How do you do, Sir? Thank God you're safe.

SIR BERTRAM: And thanks, for holding the fort. Not the best introduction for you, I'm afraid. Let's see the damage.

The two men walk round – SIR BERTRAM *becoming visibly more and more angry at what he sees. He gives tight smiles and brief words of encouragement and sympathy to the staff, still sheltering on the first floor. He then turns to* CAMPBELL.

SIR BERTRAM: Campbell, I'm off to the Ministry for Foreign Affairs, if I can borrow a vehicle from the Australian Embassy next door. It's imperative that I register a formal protest, at the highest level I can reach. This was a government-inspired, government-controlled, demonstration. As soon as I'm back,

I'll take you to the Residence, to settle in and meet Lady
Budely.

ROBERT CAMPBELL: Yes Sir.

SIR BERTRAM: Meanwhile, send an *en clair* reporting telegram to
London. Keep it short and factual. No comment or sob stuff.
Stiff upper. You know the sort of thing. I don't need to see it –
just get it off, straight away.

ROBERT CAMPBELL: Very good, Sir.

Ext. Phnom Penh International Airport. Ten days later.

*The British Ambassador and his wife are about to leave
Cambodia, for good. A handful of diplomats from other Embassies
(Australian, US, French, German, Japanese) are present. Also:*
CAMPBELL, *alongside the new* MILITARY ATTACHE *and the new*
VICE-CONSUL. *Much shaking of hands, and artificial cheerfulness.*
THE AMBASSADOR *speaks to* CAMPBELL *last.*

SIR BERTRAM: (*lowering his voice and speaking confidentially*)
Good luck, Campbell. God knows when or whether there will
be another Ambassador to replace me. Cambodia is becoming
the graveyard of diplomatic reputations.

ROBERT CAMPBELL: It's not your fault, Sir. But you and Lady
Budely do deserve a break, and a calmer spell, somewhere
civilised. Don't forget us, back in Cambodia. I'll always be
grateful for expert advice, from afar.

SIR BERTRAM: Good of you, Campbell. But, frankly I don't think
so. I've pretty well shot my bolt. From now on, it will be your

call. Watch the King, like a hawk. Otherwise just heed your canny Scots instincts. But now, goodbye from us both.

ROBERT CAMPBELL: Goodbye, Sir Bertram, Lady Budely. Safe journey.

The passengers embark, the doors close, the aircraft taxis out onto the runway. The foreign diplomats disperse, with the exception of the Australian Ambassador, NOEL RANKIN, *a tanned and grizzled figure of about 60.* RANKIN *is Cambridge-educated, but speaks with a slight Aussie accent. Occasionally lapses into 'Strine'.*

ROBERT CAMPBELL: Thank you for coming to the airport, Sir. The Budelys clearly appreciated it. But please don't stay. I'll just stand here a little longer and watch the plane out of sight – the correct protocol, I believe.

NOEL RANKIN: First, I am not "Sir". Just call me "Noel". As far as I'm concerned, from now on, you're "Bob". Second, old "BB" was a man I had real time for. He could be a stuffy old sod. But he had guts. So, I'll wait with you. Then, why don't we drive back into town together? Send your driver home. There's a lot to talk about.

CAMPBELL *gives him a steady look, to see whether he is serious. Then nods gratefully. They watch the aircraft take off, rise, dwindle to a silver dot in the blue sky, and then disappear from sight.*

Int. The Australian Ambassador's large, black limousine.

RANKIN *is driving himself, Aussie-style.* CAMPBELL *in the front seat beside him, having dismissed his own chauffeured Austin 'Princess'. The two men head into town.*

NOEL RANKIN: Where to, Bob? Have you taken over the Residence, yet?

ROBERT CAMPBELL: Yes. As from this moment, it's mine. I'm in – just. Haven't properly unpacked yet. Heavy luggage won't be here till Friday, by airfreight. Private car's already on its way by sea from Singapore; should be here in ten days.

NOEL RANKIN: It's a nice house, your Residence – traditional French Colonial. And in a quiet quarter. The mob won't go that way. Too close to the French Embassy – and the French have got some clout in Cambodia, at the moment.

ROBERT CAMPBELL: Reckon I've seen enough of street mobs, after last week. Expect you have, too. Your Chancery is down the boulevard from ours, after all.

NOEL RANKIN: What're you going to do, to square the place up?

ROBERT CAMPBELL: Still got a lot of archive burning to get through. I want our confidential holdings reduced to the barest minimum, just in case there's a repeat performance. As it was, we were damned lucky to have avoided a security breach.

NOEL RANKIN: I don't think they wanted your secrets – they were just out to humiliate the British Government. But you're right to be on the safe side. What about the state of the buildings and grounds, though? We don't want you Poms letting the boulevard down.

ROBERT CAMPBELL: Obviously, we'll finish clearing up the débris, get the windows back in and apply a lick of paint.

NOEL RANKIN: And all those wrecked vehicles? The private cars of your expat. staff?

ROBERT CAMPBELL: Sir Bertram wanted them left where they are, to embarrass the Cambodian authorities. Something for the international TV cameras to focus on. Sort of tourist attraction.

NOEL RANKIN: Typical of old "BB". Big psychological mistake, cobber, in my view. Takes no account of the Oriental mind.

ROBERT CAMPBELL: Meaning?

NOEL RANKIN: Listen to this. When my cook came to tell me she'd just lost her daughter to meningitis, she took care to seem to be laughing it off. Callous? Indifferent? Of course not. She just didn't want the evil spirits to think that she was rattled – in case they were tempted to come back and grab her, too.

ROBERT CAMPBELL: Noel, I'm not quite sure if I ……..

NOEL RANKIN: I'll explain. Among ordinary unsophisticated Cambodians, keeping the wrecked cars on public view simply causes you lot to lose face. Far from shaming Cambodia, it shames Britannia. Because it proclaims your weakness. Far better give the Chancery a complete make-over. Pretend the mob action never took place. Above all, you have to smile, not scowl. Old "BB", was a good bloke and all that. But he just looked too bloody glum. In this country, it doesn't help.

ROBERT CAMPBELL: Interesting. *(With slight sarcasm)* You obviously know the form better than most of us. *(Long pause).* Any other psycho-political tips, while you are about it?

NOEL RANKIN: Yeah! You're a new face, a young man, a good-looking guy, a creature of the 'Swinging Sixties', and all that jazz. So, just be your age, which is half mine. If I were you, mate, I'd turn myself into the giddy "Playboy Chargé d'Affaires".

ROBERT CAMPBELL: Meaning what, exactly?

NOEL RANKIN: Meaning put yourself about. Go to all the right parties, the best nightclubs. Dress up like a pox doctor's clerk. Dance until dawn. Be seen to be having fun – even if it's only on the surface. Even if it hurts. But behind that smokescreen, build your contacts. Aggressively. At the top. Come back fighting. Be British.

ROBERT CAMPBELL: *(Deciding to confess his true feelings and be damned)* Look Noel, I didn't ask to come here. I'd much rather be back in Washington, dealing with things closer to home, things that really matter. I'd be the first to cheer, if London decided to close the British Embassy altogether.

NOEL RANKIN: Understandable, at the personal level. And I grant that the future of this country will be determined by factors over which you have no control. Attitude of Red China. Viet Cong resilience. All the rest.

ROBERT CAMPBELL: And the US, too.

NOEL RANKIN: The US, too! I don't like their conduct of the war in Vietnam. Frankly, in this neck of the woods, these days, being America's ally is like finding yourself in a very small sitting room with a very large friendly dog. He means well, but every time he wags his tail, half the china goes flying. As London found out, with their peace initiative for Cambodia.

ROBERT CAMPBELL: So, what am I here for, Noel? Be frank.

Because me, I haven't a clue!

NOEL RANKIN: Because – for maybe just a short period – the Brits can still influence things, one way or the other. To save Cambodia. You happen to be standing at the centre of the seesaw.

ROBERT CAMPBELL: At the still point of the turning world, you mean, in the words of T.S. Eliott?

NOEL RANKIN: Don't come all Cambridge with me, mate. I was there too – *and* got a First. But there's everything still to play for, to keep Cambodia out of the war. And the individual can still count. If his face fits. Which is where you come in, as the new Brit on the street, in Phnom Penh. As I said just now, it will depend on your 'image', your *figura*, as the Italians would say. No more long faces, BB-style!

ROBERT CAMPBELL: OK. I'll think about it. (*Long pause, while he looks out of the window, as the car enters central Phnom Penh. Then, thoughtfully:*) Maybe I might just give it a try?

Int. The British Embassy Chancery, the next day.

A staff meeting. For the first time since the Ambassador's departure, CAMPBELL *is in the chair and visibly in charge, attempting to be confident and clear-cut. The others include the just arrived new* MILITARY ATTACHÉ, *the* BRITISH COUNCIL REPRESENTATIVES *attached to the Embassy,* THE OUTGOING CONSUL, TWO VICE-CONSULS, THE DIPLOMATIC WIRELESS OFFICER, THE ARCHIVIST. *A mixture of the Old Guard (expecting to leave shortly) and the New (not yet all present). Also two elegant,*

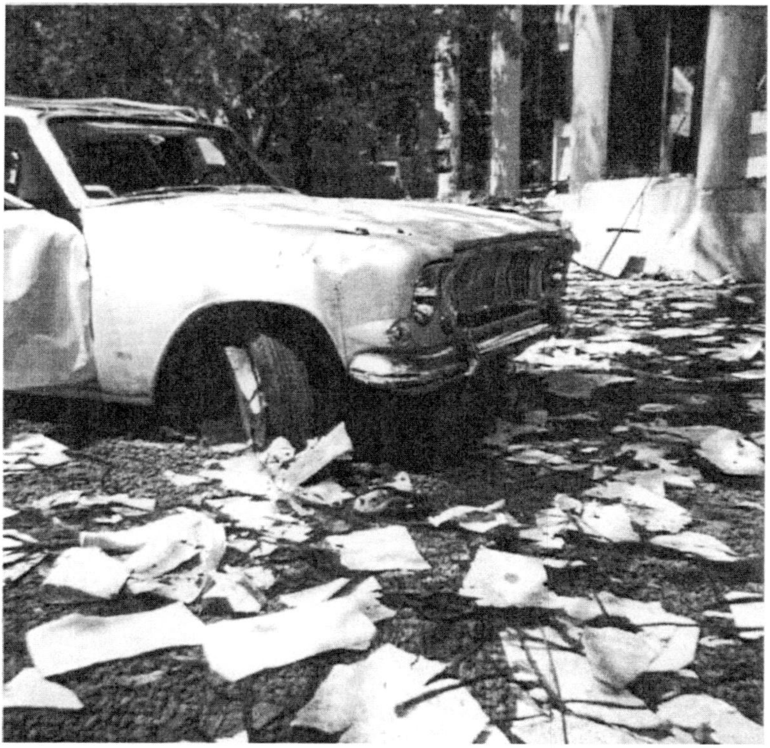

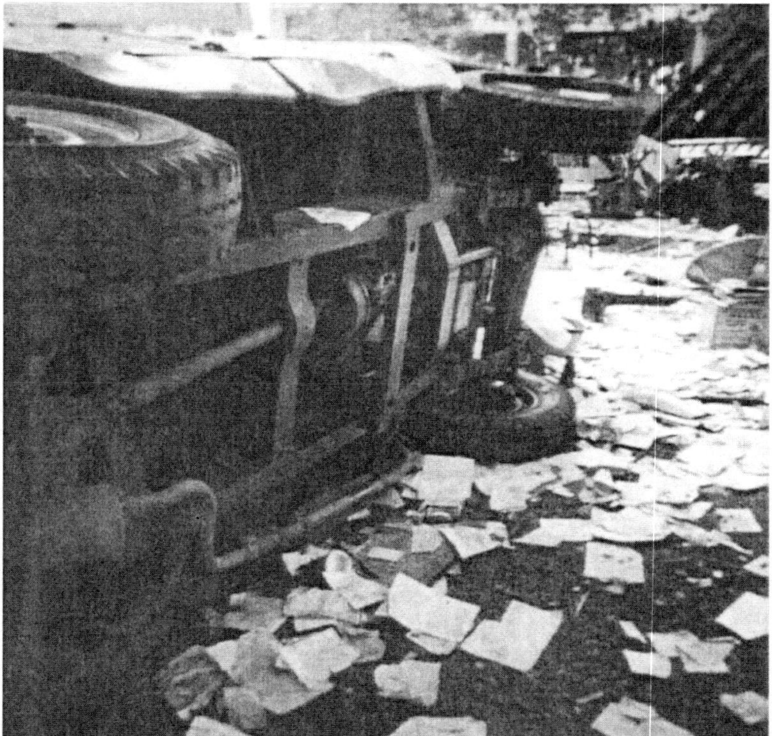

youngish, good-looking, Cambodian staffers: the (male) PRESS SECRETARY *and the (female)* TRANSLATOR.

CONSUL: But H.E. specifically said that the wrecked cars should stay where they are.

ROBERT CAMPBELL: Maybe. But Sir Bertram left me complete discretion. Sorry, but I want the cars carted away, tomorrow. They're a bad advertisement. Make us look as if we are wallowing in it. Let's show them that we're back in business, as if nothing had happened.

The TWO CAMBODIAN STAFFERS *exchange glances and nod.*

Ext. The Chancery compound, the following day.

The wrecked cars are being winched onto lorries, to be removed. In the sweltering heat, Cambodian coolies are clearing up wrecked furniture, picking up broken glass and rubbish. Builders are at work putting in new windows and repainting walls. In the backyard, sweating in the heat, British staff are feeding classified documents into incinerators. Dust and smoke everywhere.
CAMPBELL *everywhere, too, lending a hand.*

Int. The British Ambassador's (now Campbell's) Residence, the following week.

The last of the Embassy's 'Old Guard' has left Cambodia. The new, skeleton, staff are all now in post. The new Military Attaché and his wife are in their early forties; the new British Council Representative and his French wife, in their mid-thirties.

Otherwise, half a dozen young officials, without dependents, like Campbell. The Chargé d'Affaires has asked everyone round to the Residence for a buffet supper and a pep talk.

ROBERT CAMPBELL: Welcome, all of you, to Phnom Penh! We're the new Embassy team. The "A" team – though that's hard to credit! (*People smile, politely*). I'm as new to all this as you are. But I'd like to make one or two things clear.

First, I didn't volunteer to be Her Britannic Majesty's Chargé d'Affaires in Cambodia. I was simply "volunteered". The same has happened to some of you. Me, I'd rather be back in the Washington Embassy. Phnom Penh doesn't matter too much, I think, in the world order of things. Not to the UK. And the natives are not exactly friendly! At the moment, at least. Frankly, if it had been left to me, I'd have closed this Embassy altogether and had done with it. But the Prime Minister and the Foreign Secretary, in their wisdom, happen to have decided otherwise. And that's what matters to us.

Second, I'm not whingeing. I don't want you to whinge, either. It's what we signed up for, when we first joined the Service. Challenge, Adventure, Hard Work. All that. So, let's get on with it.

Third, I want us all to have some fun, too, while we're about it. The Embassy may have been attacked. The future may be uncertain. But we shan't be down-hearted. The eyes of the locals are upon us. Take your cue from me. I'll be working hard, round the clock. But, as far as the Cambodians will be concerned, I'll also be my age. I hope you will all do the same.

Last thing, don't hesitate to come to me, with any personal problems you may run into. I'm here to look after you. Despite my relative youth, think of me as avuncular. "Uncle Robert, he's true blue; Uncle Bob, he cares for you!" That sort of thing. *(The others have been listening carefully, initially even a little anxiously. But they begin to relax and smile.* CAMPBELL *raises his glass.)* So, here's to us! And remember. In years to come, we shall look back to these days in Phnom Penh, and we shall call them "the good old days"! And now, if you'll follow me into the dining room, a spot of supper awaits.

Ext. The forecourt of the British Embassy Chancery. Two weeks later. Early evening.

CAMPBELL *is getting into his newly delivered, white sports car, after collecting some local currency from the office. He is wearing a tuxedo, with an orchid in the buttonhole, evidently on his way to somewhere special. The new* MILITARY ATTACHÉ *is seeing his Australian colleague out of the building, after a courtesy call. The former says 'Wow!'. The latter gives a disrespectful wolf whistle.*

BRITISH MILITARY ATTACHÉ: I say, Bob. Look at you! Quite the dashing young subaltern!

ROBERT CAMPBELL Actually, gentlemen, it's all the Aussie Ambassador's idea. I'm now Great Britain's new 'Swinging Sixties' Playboy Chargé d'Affaires! All singing. All dancing. Trying to look cuddly and harmless.

BRITISH MILITARY ATTACHÉ: You know what you're doing, I suppose. Good luck to you, anyway. I only wish I were still your age – and had your sports car.

ROBERT CAMPBELL: I'd swap it for your Armoured Personal Carrier, any day, Colonel. Toodle-oo!

CAMPBELL *drives off, spinning the wheels in the gravel.*

CAMPBELL'S NEWLY ARRIVED PA: (*coming on the scene as* CAMPBELL *leaves*) Dishy, isn't he, Colonel?

BRITISH MILITARY ATTACHÉ: *And* well heeled. *And* well connected. *And* on his way to 'The Top'. *And* knows it. Also, I begin to suspect, quite ruthless about it. I'd handle with care, Barbara, if I were you.

Ext. A very smart, exclusive, open-air nightclub, on the banks of the Mekong river, later that evening.

CAMPBELL, *in his white tuxedo, leans against a balustrade, looking at the beautiful people. He smiles at a striking Euro-Asiatic girl in a small group. She returns his smile.* CAMPBELL *beckons her to join him, for a glass of champagne. She shakes her head, but waves him over, to join her own party. Polite introductions, in French. She is* MARTINE LEFÈVRE, *with her father, a Brigadier General in the French army. Two more introductions – a Cambodian Court official and a senior police officer. The remaining figure is a petite, exquisite and quite mysterious young woman. The Courtier whispers in* CAMPBELL*'s ear that she is* H.R.H. THE PRINCESS DEVI SRI, *the King's daughter. Conversation is initially in French, then switches to English.*

GENERAL LEFEVRE: (*speaking in French: subtitles as follows*)
Your Royal Highness, may I present the new British Chargé d'Affaires, M. .... (*after prompting*) M. Campbell.

CAMPBELL *bows and whispers something ultra-polite. There is some small talk. Then, the* PRINCESS *looks at her watch, makes her excuses. She and her two Cambodian escorts leave.*

ROBERT CAMPBELL: Was that *really* the King's daughter? His *favourite* daughter? The one that's the Prima Ballerina of the *Royal Corps de Ballet*?

GENERAL LEFEVRE: Indeed it was – and one of my daughter's best friends, as it happens. My late wife and the mother of that Princess were related. Went to school together.

MARTINE LEFEVRE: M. Campbell, you speak good French.

GENERAL LEFEVRE: For an Englishman, that's rare.

MARTINE LEFEVRE: You must excuse my father's directness. A bit outmoded, in the present day and age. Just understand that he is a *military* man. The Head of our Military Mission to Cambodia, no less!

ROBERT CAMPBELL: I have the greatest respect for military men, Madame. Nothing wrong, about being direct, either. My father was a Company Commander in the British army during the war, and I followed him into his Regiment, for my National Service. But that was some time ago. Life has moved on a bit, since then.

MARTINE LEFEVRE: (*switching to English*) Indeed. And, like you, Mr Campbell, I too belong to the modern world. Guess what? I even speak *English*. Daddy and I actually lived in London for a bit, till recently – he was attached to your Ministry of Defence. By the way, I'm not 'Madame' but 'Martine'. And your first name is ....?

ROBERT CAMPBELL: Robert. But everyone calls me Bob.

GENERAL LEFEVRE: Which was your Regiment, Mr Campbell?

ROBERT CAMPBELL: The Black Watch. I was with them in Korea.

GENERAL LEFEVRE: (*looks closely at* CAMPBELL, *warming to him, and nods*) Actually, I remember you: weren't you on the Defence Desk in the Foreign Office? Those meetings, during the Berlin crisis?

MARTINE LEFEVRE: Who cares about such things, daddy? Think of the pop song, "All You Need Is Love".

ROBERT CAMPBELL: Absolutely! And: 'Give Peace a Chance'!

MARTINE LEFEVRE: Yes, even in primitive Cambodia, we've just about heard of The Beatles.

ROBERT CAMPBELL: Personally, I'm always ready to "Give Peace a Chance". Sadly, though, international relations are not always quite so simple. The General would agree, I'm sure?

GENERAL LEFEVRE: (*turning to his daughter*) Time to be off home now, dear – Her Royal Highness no longer has need of us.

MARTINE *shakes* CAMPBELL *by the hand, with a smile.*

MARTINE LEFEVRE: Goodnight... er, ... *Bob*. Expect we'll see you again, soon. It's a small town.

GENERAL LEFEVRE: Goodnight, Campbell.

Ext. The Mekong river. The British Embassy's *maison flottante.*

A traditional wooden structure, with thatched roof, built on a large wooden raft, anchored to the bank of the Mekong river. There are staff and changing rooms on the landward side, and a kitchen. Facing the river is a large, open-sided veranda. Railings all round, except for a set of broad wooden steps which lead down into the water, where a sleek outboard motor boat is moored. CAMPBELL, *his* MILITARY ATTACHÉ *and his* PA *are entertaining some members of the Diplomatic Corps, including* GENERAL LEFÈVRE *and his daughter. Champagne is being served, by the Cambodian servants.*

ROBERT CAMPBELL: (*to the Lefèvres*) This is our new Embassy houseboat, complete with launch, for water-skiing.

GENERAL LEFEVRE: Either you are very rich, M. Campbell, or the British Government are very generous.

ROBERT CAMPBELL: More the latter. I told London that times were hard and Embassy morale needed boosting – and I think that my M.A. would agree that détente on water-skis is a military necessity. Isn't that so Colonel?

MILITARY ATTACHE; Absolutely, Bob.

GENERAL LEFEVRE *laughs, visibly unbending.*

ROBERT CAMPBELL: (*to the General*) Care to come out on the water skis with me, *Mon Général*? My motorboat can pull two.

MARTINE LEFEVRE: (*interrupting, speaking to her father*) Papa, what would Mummy have said? Just think of your rank, your dignity, your age! Let me go in your place. (*Turning to*

Campbell's PA). Do you think I could borrow a costume, or something? Would you possibly mind?

ROBERT CAMPBELL: Barbara, do you think you could find something suitably skimpy, please?

The PA smiles and nods. Takes MARTINE into a changing room. She comes out in a borrowed bikini, a slant-eyed beauty – long legs, a French figure and a darkish, honeyed Cambodian complexion. CAMPBELL has changed into his Hawaiian shorts. They each don life jackets and go out in the launch, driven by CAMPBELL'S PA. A cheer goes up from the houseboat, as CAMPBELL and MARTINE are towed upright and move off in a flurry of spray. They weave in and out, in a wide circle. The MILITARY ATTACHÉ watches through his binoculars; passes them to THE GENERAL.

MILITARY ATTACHÉ: A handsome young couple, General.

GENERAL LEFEVRE: Don't say that, Colonel. It makes me jealous.

Since my beloved Cambodian partner passed away, Martine is all I have.

Int. The King's Private Palace.

The King's favourite daughter, PRINCESS DEVI SRI, has recently become engaged. A celebratory dinner dance is under way, attended by a selection of bigwigs: Cambodian Cabinet Ministers; foreign Ambassadors; Court advisers; cultural attachés; local newspaper editors.

CAMPBELL, *as a new arrival in Phnom Penh and the British Chargé d'Affaires, is presented to THE KING, who shakes his hand,* *enquires politely after the British Ambassador, asking when he will return to Phnom Penh. (*THE KING *has not been told, yet, that the Ambassador has been definitively withdrawn and will not be coming back).* CAMPBELL *replies, non-committally, that Sir Bertram is still on 'home leave'.*

During the reception, while the Court orchestra plays chamber music, CAMPBELL *is being taken round the throng by the Australian Ambassador,* NOEL RANKIN, *and introduced to VIPs. Among them, four men who will be important later:* PRINCE MONIVONG, *the Prime Minister (who enters a secret pact with Campbell to re-start the peace process; but who is eventually murdered by Pol Pot);*DAN McGUIRE, *the Irish-American head of the "Cultural Foundation" (who is really the local head of the CIA; he gives Campbell valuable information and advice; but is eventually declared 'persona non grata' by the King, and expelled from the country); the ultra right-wing Head of the Cambodian Armed Forces,* GENERAL LON NOL *(later to overthrow the King in a coup d'etat, only to suffer subsequent military defeat at the hands of Pol Pot, and to die in exile in Hawaii); and the leftist French journalist* MAURICE LeBRUN, *who has become a royal special advisor. (Although sympathetic to Mao Tse-tung, and no admirer of the West in general and the US in particular,* LeBRUN *nevertheless supports the peace process, and establishes a cautiously constructive relationship with Campbell, behind the scenes; he dies, later, in suspicious circumstances – probably murdered on the orders of General Lon Nol).*

PRINCE MONIVONG: (*in French*) Good evening, M. le Chargé

d'Affaires. A rare privilege to meet an Anglo-Saxon diplomat socially, these days. Please convey my best wishes to your Ambassador, when next you see him.

As they move on, the Australian Ambassador whispers:

NOEL RANKIN: The PM is personally well disposed, but bound by the King's edict that Cambodians must not mix with British or American diplomats, socially. Remember, you're supposed to be 'in Coventry'. Occasions like this, at the Palace, are the only permitted exception.

GENERAL LON NOL: (*slightly drunk, speaking demotic French, with a Khmer accent*) Evening. What's the latest on your war in Vietnam? The less Viets on the planet, the better! (*On correction by the Australian Ambassador, that* CAMPBELL *is British, not American*). Sorry! (*Laughs heartily*). The English should be out there in South Vietnam, too, like during the Korean war.

ROBERT CAMPBELL: I was, General. In Korea. Quite a party.

GENERAL LON NOL *looks appraisingly, then nods and turns away.*

NOEL RANKIN: (*whispering in* CAMPBELL*'s ear*) General Lon Nol is racist: in effect, pathologically anti-Vietnamese of all political colours and none. Also, quite thick – and drinks too much whisky. Now come and meet this interesting American.

DAN McGUIRE: Greetings. So. You're a Campbell? Me, I'm American. I'm Irish. I'm Catholic too, so I am. And I've never forgiven the Brits, for all their colonial misdeeds in the Emerald Isle. Can't stand the Scots, in particular! *(*CAMPBELL, *unimpressed, grins broadly.)* But, just for the time being, I'll pass that over. God and Mary with us, but we're both of us in deep doo-doo, you and me, right now in Phnom Penh! So, we'd better speak to each other. Welcome to the doghouse (*slapping* CAMPBELL *on the shoulder*).

NOEL RANKIN: (*moving on, still whispering*) Highly acute, under all that Irish Blarney. He's really CIA – the Cultural Foundation is just cover. But don't let on that I told you. 'Top Secret' and all that!

MAURICE LeBRUN: (*middle-aged, straggly moustache, socially ill at ease, wears an ill-fitting dinner jacket, with clip-on bow tie, slightly askew. They speak French together*) Monsieur. Very content to meet you. How do you do? (*Stiffly, avoiding direct eye contact with* CAMPBELL). Permit me to introduce myself. Maurice LeBrun. I have the honour to be the King's special advisor on foreign policy, part-time. Also, I write for *L'Humanité*. One regrets, of course, the fate of your last Ambassador. His intentions, personally, were positive; his conduct, correct. The Cambodian Government might have done better to direct the rioters to 10 Downing Street, instead!

We shall no doubt be in touch, from time to time, Monsieur. But kindly do not telephone me – I'll call you. I have no ambition to be thought a running dog of Anglo-American capitalism.

ROBERT CAMPBELL: I'll try to remember. But why don't we meet over a Pernod, some time, at the Foreign Correspondent's Club? You'll be able to tell me about your days with Special Operations Executive, in Vichy France. I'm told you're still remembered with admiration.

MAURICE LeBRUN: (*surprised, but gratified*) *Tiens!* So you know about that? Yes – they were good days, working together against the Nazis and the fascists. Possibly we could find common ground again, you and I? On the King's terms, naturally.

NOEL RANKIN: (*as they have moved away from everyone else*) Onya, cobber! You're a 'beaudy'! (*Winks at* CAMPBELL. *Reverts to normal English*). I didn't know about the S.O.E. connection. Anyway, he's the latest *eminence grise* at Court. Everyone except the King mistrusts him – even the French Ambassador. LeBrun probably even mistrusts himself. He's a card-carrying Communist, of the pro-Chinese kind. I'd sup with a very long spoon, mate, if I were you.

CAMPBELL *catches sight of* MARTINE, *goes over to her with relief. They promise each other a dance, after dinner. He shakes hands with her friends – including the King's daughter, who recognises him, and to whom he bows.*

Int. The ballroom, an hour later.

Dinner is over and the dance band has started to play. THE KING *conducts a romantic Cambodian love song of his own composition, the words huskily breathed into a microphone by the band's crooner. The Court applaud, dutifully.* THE KING *hands over the baton to the regular conductor, who – greatly daring - opens the dancing with Chubby Checker's 'Let's twist again, like we did last summer'. The tune is evidently completely new in Cambodia. No one knows what to do. People look puzzled and hang back from the dance floor.*

CAMPBELL *knows Chubby Checker from Washington, having learnt to dance The Twist two months previously. He walks across the floor towards the diminutive* PRINCESS DEVI SRI, *who smiles.* CAMPBELL *bows, asks her fiancé (a Prince) for permission, then sweeps her onto the floor. After initial bewilderment,* THE PRINCESS *catches the rhythm; begins twisting elegantly – with growing confidence and enthusiasm. No one joins them; everyone watches; they dance alone, at the centre of a wide circle.*

The music stops. THE KING *takes the microphone.*

THE KING: (*in French*) Ladies and gentlemen. That was a magnificent sight. (*Giggles*). We hereby declare the British Chargé d'Affaires to be "The Number One Twister of Cambodia"!

Applause. The orchestra plays a ragged fanfare. A chamberlain is sent running for a prize, which the King hands over, shaking with amiable laughter. CAMPBELL *bows, and rejoins the throng. The band starts to play a Cha-Cha-Cha. The dance floor fills.* CAMPBELL *shows his prize to those around him, before handing it to a Palace footman for safekeeping. He then seeks out* MARTINE *and they join the other dancers.*

Int. The Royal Palace, half an hour later.

CAMPBELL, MARTINE, PRINCESS DEVI SRI *and her fiancé are chatting enthusiastically, during a pause in the dancing. The conversation is in French.*

MARTINE LEFEVRE: How well you dance, Bob. What a ....? What was the expression I learned in London? Yes ...... (*in English*) what a 'Debs Delight'!

PRINCESS DEVI SRI: Never heard that English expression before. But you are a 'Beau Sabreur' and Papa obviously likes you. Unlike boring old Ambassador Budely!

An Equerry slides up to THE KING, *grovels and whispers something.* PRIME MINISTER, GENERAL LON NOL *and* MAURICE LeBRUN *are urgently summoned, to confer on one side with* THE KING. *The latter then advances to the podium and takes the microphone.*

THE KING: (*in French*) Highnesses, Excellences. Sadly, we must bring this evening to a close. Affairs of State require our immediate attention.

Commotion and sotto voce hubbub. THE KING *and his entourage, including* THE PRINCESS *and* HER FIANCÉ, *withdraw hastily, after which the guests begin to leave the Palace, conducted by the Major Domo and other Palace flunkeys.* CAMPBELL *seeks out* GENERAL LEFÈVRE *in the lobby, as they wait for their limousines.*

ROBERT CAMPBELL: What's up, *Mon Général*?

GENERAL LEFEVRE: Not quite sure yet, Robert. Apparently a frontier incident. The Americans have flown over from Vietnam and flattened a Cambodian village near the border.......

Int. The British Residence, half an hour later.

CAMPBELL *in his study, on the telephone, replying to a call from a senior official in the Cambodian Foreign Ministry.*

SENIOR CAMBODIAN OFFICIAL: *(Stiff and slightly stilted)*
Excellency, what took place today was a major violation of Cambodian territorial integrity by United States forces. We are launching a formal complaint to the Security Council of the United Nations.

ROBERT CAMPBELL: I will so inform London. What can you tell me, about the situation on the ground?

SENIOR CAMBODIAN OFFICIAL: The village has been extensively damaged. About thirty villagers killed, many more injured. Half the buildings destroyed.

ROBERT CAMPBELL: Will there be external verification?

SENIOR CAMBODIAN OFFICIAL: The International Control Commission are to conduct an investigation. It will take place tomorrow. The ICC will be accompanied by a representative of the US Embassy. We look to the British and the USSR Embassies to be represented. Also observers from certain other Embassies, including that of Australia, in view of Australian participation in the war in Vietnam.

Int. The Chancery in the British Embassy, early the next morning.

CAMPBELL *'s office. A meeting with two or three of his staff. News agency reports and local newspapers spread over the desk. The radio on Campbell's desk carries a French language news bulletin, just ending.* CAMPBELL *switches it off.*

ROBERT CAMPBELL: So that's it. Not nice. Not the end of the world either. The Foreign Ministry were in touch with me, late last night. They want us and the Russians down there; the Americans and Australians as well. All as observers. Where's my Military Attaché?

ROBERT CAMPBELL'S PA: Colonel Russell won't be back from the Singapore Conference till tomorrow morning, I'm afraid.

ROBERT CAMPBELL: Then I suppose I'll have to go in his place. Can't avoid it, in the circs.

VICE-CONSUL: Both the Embassy Land Rovers are in the dock.

ROBERT CAMPBELL: (*to his PA*) Barbara, find out, please, if the Australians will take me with them? I don't want to cadge a lift with the US Embassy. Risk of guilt, by association! (*Wry laughter. The meeting breaks up*).

Ext. The road to the frontier with Vietnam.

A convoy of assorted civilian vehicles, foreign Embassy and official Cambodian, is heading through the rice fields towards the frontier. CAMPBELL *is in the Australian Military Attaché's Land Rover. Both men are in civilian clothes, as indeed is everyone except the uniformed Cambodian police escort.*

THE AUSTRALIAN M.A.: Not a hot pursuit operation, from what I can gather, Bob. No way an attack on some sort of secret Vietcong base on Cambodian soil, either. Thereabouts, it's just a bloody peasant community ...... typical Cambodian village, four kilometres in from the frontier.

ROBERT CAMPBELL: Yep! But the place got bombed. How come?

THE AUSTRALIAN M.A.: Navigational error, maybe, in the heat of the moment. Or maybe even just some trigger happy guys. The Yanks don't like "Gooks", of any description. Yankee pilots? They're usually either green or yellow. In this case, probably just inexperienced and over-excited kids.

Ext. Cambodian village.

The column of vehicles is parked on the highway outside. The Cambodian police escort stays with the column, leaving the civilian officials from the Ministry of the Interior to lead the foreign diplomats around. They enter the village, made up of wooden buildings on stilts, roofed with banana leaf thatching. Much evidence of bomb damage. Dead water buffaloes lie on their backs, feet rigid, bellies extended with gas. Some houses have been burnt to the ground, by napalm. The petrol smell – and that of human and animal dead bodies – is heavy in the damp tropical air. The corpses of some Cambodian peasants lie side by side, covered in rattan to keep the flies off; the occasional arm, leg or even head poking out. The observers, led by the Cambodian civilians, walk round the village, taking notes and photographs, watched by the sullen-faced village survivors. No sign of military installations or weapons, either in the village or in its immediate vicinity.

Ext. Outside the village.

The Vietnamese frontier, according to the Australian's map, lies nearby, along a range of low hills on the eastern horizon. From beyond that horizon, the sounds of war – the crump of bombs, the distant sound of heavy machine guns (like tearing calico). Clouds of smoke are visible, and military aircraft circling in the distance. One of these, a US Air Force Skyraider, detaches itself, crosses the frontier and over-flies the village, attracted by the unwonted activity on the ground. The pilot banks, to get a better look, then turns away.

THE AUSTRALIAN M.A.: He doesn't like us, Bob. All us white faces in civvies. Bet he thinks you're Ho Chi Minh and I'm a Vietcong attack column.

ROBERT CAMPBELL: Surely not. He's just making a 'recce'.

The Skyraider turns in a wide arc, enters a shallow dive and makes a run on the village.

THE AUSTRALIAN M.A.: No such luck. (*Yells out to the rest of the group*). Watch out! He's gonna open fire! Spread out!! Dive for cover!!!

The others have already been following the aircraft's manoeuvres, rooted to the spot. Then, as one, they disperse off the road, in different directions, diving into various irrigation ditches.

THE AUSTRALIAN M.A.: Come on, Bob. Move yourself! Into this ditch!!

They jump into a deep and muddy watercourse, beside the track. Some other observers pile in, ahead, behind, and on top. CAMPBELL *closes his eyes, lying prone in the bottom of the ditch. The Skyraider weaves slightly from side to side and then opens fire briefly with its machine guns. Bits of sugar palm fly about and there are puffs of dust on the surface of the track. But no one in the ditches gets hit. The aircraft – clearly now out of ammo, at the end of its mission, and probably running low on fuel – soars upward, levels, and flies back over the frontier, heading for Saigon. One by one, the diplomatic observers and their Cambodian minders crawl back onto the road, dust themselves down and make a run for their vehicles.* CAMPBELL *looks in dismay at his mudded white tropical suit; picks up his Panama hat – complete with Cambridge College ribbon – jams it firmly on his head and falls in step with the* AUSTRALIAN MILITARY ATTACHÉ. *The latter, annoyingly, refuses to be in any hurry; he strolls along nonchalantly – the last, with* CAMPBELL, *to rejoin the vehicles, most of which are now heading off at speed back to Phnom Penh.*

THE AUSTRALIAN M.A.: Shittabrick, mate, what do you think we looked like, down there, flat out in that bloody ditch, like 'Goannas' drinking?

ROBERT CAMPBELL: Don't know what a 'Goanna' is. But we were absolutely sitting ducks. Thank God he couldn't shoot straight.

THE AUSTRALIAN M.A.: Yeah! Like I said, mate. American pilots? Either they're green or they're yella. That one was *green*!

CAMPBELL *suddenly reaches a conclusion which is to guide his* actions for the remainder of his mission to Cambodia. It is a moment of psychological transition.

ROBERT CAMPBELL: (*speaking aloud, but quietly, almost to himself*). This has simply got to stop. This whole, neutral, peaceful, happy country is absolutely on the brink. We're supposed to be Co-effing-President of the Geneva Convention on Indo-China. We've got to try again, with that Peace Plan. If it works, these people have a chance of surviving the war in Vietnam. If it fails, it's curtains for Cambodia. *Curtains*.

A series of locations. Scenes without words.

Voice over: ROBERT CAMPBELL *starts a crash programme, to get to grips with a new job, in a new country. He begins by reading everything he can lay his hands on. (Pictures of Campbell late at night at the Residence, immersed in a pile of books about Cambodian history, culture, customs, anthropology, etc). He sits, metaphorically, at the feet of "Old Hands" in the expatriate French community – businessmen, engineers, journalists, who have lived among the Cambodians for years. (Pictures of* CAMPBELL *in the slightly seedy, very French, 'Bar Jean', over drinks with the habitual clientele; at smart restaurants, with more up-market figures.) Always asking questions; getting his interlocutors to unbutton and explain – as the French love to, when challenged. Using his Hong Kong and Singapore connections, he calls on top businessmen in the Chinese community, the people who make the economy tick. In his spare time, he moves in Martine's charmed circle of friends, seeking her out whenever he can. At her insistence, he starts to acquire basic Khmer, in lessons from a US-educated Buddhist Abbott, a favourite at Court. (The latter, with shaven head and saffron robes, seated opposite* CAMPBELL *in the open-air school room normally used for the instruction of young novice monks. Switch to dialogue with the teacher).*

ROBERT CAMPBELL: Holiness, I must be able to say the following, if I get caught by a mob. "Good day, how do you do? I am not American – I am British. The Head of the Embassy in Phnom Penh, Cambodia".

ABBOT: Very good. Repeat, after me ...... (*begins lesson*).

Int. The Headquarters of 'Radio Khmer'. Martine's office.

CAMPBELL *is paying a courtesy call on the State Broadcaster, and takes the opportunity to drop in, to see* MARTINE.

MARTINE LEFEVRE: And, in addition to all that, and by the way, and if you please – how's your *Khmer*? Is that old Buddhist Abbot of yours any good, as tutor? Own up!

ROBERT CAMPBELL: Really rather good. My pronunciation isn't yet all that hot. But I *can* say the basics. Like "How do you do? How's your father? Where's the loo?"

MARTINE LEFEVRE: Well, we'll take all that for granted. But I'm concerned about your Anglo-Saxon *mis*pronunciation of our vowels and consonants. Now, practice makes perfect – as they used to say, at the 'Monkey Club'. Kindly wrap your tongue around this, and say, slowly, after me: *Knjom Soûm Louk Thom Thom Sleaq Peaq, Phi-Muoy, Phong?* (CAMPBELL *attempts to speak the words, phrase by phrase*). Again! (CAMPBELL *repeats —more convincingly this time*).

ROBERT CAMPBELL: May I know what it means, please?

MARTINE LEFEVRE: It means: "Would Your Excellency kindly lower his trousers, very slowly, please!?"

ROBERT CAMPBELL: Gosh! Better not repeat that to His Holiness!

MARTINE LEFEVRE: By the way, what *do* Scotsmen wear beneath the kilt? I've always wanted to know, but never dared ask.

ROBERT CAMPBELL: There's nothing to tell! (*He pursues her round the desk*). Anyway, I'm much more interested in the Cambodian for "How much, for a fried beetle sandwich?"

MARTINE LEFEVRE: Make mine a *caviar* sandwich, please! Better lock my office door, by the way!

More scenes without words.

Voice over: ROBERT CAMPBELL *pays official calls around town. The calls on the Prime Minister, Foreign/Finance/Interior Ministers, are formal and routine, confined to protocolaire politenesses, Ministerial faces inscrutable. They are still nervous; embarrassed by what happened to the British Embassy; unsure of what to say, policy-wise; and apprehensive of the King, even though the British Embassy is now socially 'kosher' and out of Coventry, following Campbell's rehabilitation as the 'Number One Twister'.* CAMPBELL *begins to pick up the threads of local reality and put himself on the map. He has not yet, however, given evidence of diplomatic 'savvy' and operational 'street cred'. So, some of his interlocutors speak to him with a hint of condescension and over-simplification, as if to a well-intentioned but ignorant simpleton.*

Int. The French Embassy, the Ambassador's study.

THE AMBASSADOR *and* CAMPBELL *are seated in armchairs opposite each other, taking coffee.* CAMPBELL *offers to speak French. But* THE AMBASSADOR *(formerly the Number Two in New York) prefers to speak English. He is youngish, well disposed, in part English-educated (at the LSE). But irritatingly didactic.*

FRENCH AMBASSADOR: The man who really understood French Indo-China, I freely admit, was an Englishman – Sir Anthony Eden! (CAMPBELL *raises his eyebrows in interrogation*). After Dien Bien Phu, we French had to pull out. Eden struck a deal with the Russians. Vietnam was a write-off. But Laos and Cambodia, next door, had to stay neutral and constitute a buffer zone. There were to be so-called 'free elections' in Vietnam, both North and South, for 'face-saving' reasons. But everyone understood that North and South would almost certainly then be united under Ho Chi Minh.

ROBERT CAMPBELL: Things didn't quite end up that way, did they?

FRENCH AMBASSADOR: Alas, the so-called 'Domino Theory' took hold in America. Hence today's Vietnam War – bitter, entirely without hope. We French have a poor view of President Lyndon Johnson's judgement.

ROBERT CAMPBELL: As you know, Ambassador, it was Johnson who pulled the plug last autumn, on the Anglo-Soviet Peace Plan for Cambodia. I was in Washington, right at the end. There was a lot of broken glass.

FRENCH AMBASSADOR: I understand. But the project is not dead, surely? The King continues to cling to Cambodia's neutrality. The English are still in a position to help. It is a heavy responsibility, for one...... still young.

ROBERT CAMPBELL: *(slightly nettled)* You worry me, Ambassador. No doubt it's my beardless youth, as you imply.

FRENCH AMBASSADOR: (a*ware of the reaction, but persisting*) One thing more, if I may? Sooner or later, you English will have to free yourself from subordination to America. Sir Anthony Eden was a true 'European'. Britain must become 'European', once again. *(smiling)* You won't have to leave NATO, to do that!

ROBERT CAMPBELL: The US matters. But I'm a 'European' also, as it happens. And, being a Scot, I cherish *La Vieille Alliance*!

FRENCH AMBASSADOR: (*relenting*) Splendid! Shall we leave the coffee? Take a glass of champagne, instead? Here's to success in your vital new mission!

Int. The USSR Embassy, the Ambassador's office, a large red flag in the corner, and framed pictures of Soviet leaders on the wall.

THE SOVIET AMBASSADOR *is sitting behind a large, long desk,* CAMPBELL *seated opposite. The Russian is evidently out of sympathy with Indo-China, feeling a long way from home. Had served in the Soviet Embassy in London, and enjoyed it. Glad to see* CAMPBELL. *(Later, the Ambassador will become an advisor to Gorbachev, and an advocate of Perestroika.) The conversation is in English. Takes the shape of a monologue, Soviet-style – but unexpectedly open and frank.*

SOVIET AMBASSADOR: You may be surprised to hear me say this, Comrade Campbell, but I have never felt so 'European', since coming to Cambodia. It's not our part of the world at all – the climate; the Buddhism; the 'God-King'; the 'Your Highness this', the 'His Excellency that'.

To be frank, Cambodia is part of China's sphere of influence, not ours. Even before the Moscow/Beijing split, Comrade Gromyko understood that – just as your Mr Eden did. (*Campbell nods*). If London decides to get the Geneva Peace Process going again, Moscow will back you. A neutral Cambodia suits us better than a country aligned with the Americans in their ridiculous Vietnam War.

The capitalist Cambodian élite, the princely classes, the urban bourgeoisie, are pro-American simply and solely because they want to keep their privileges and make as many dollars as possible. I would expect that. But a Cambodia which abandons neutrality, and signs up with Uncle Sam, will be defeated and end up an out-and-out Chinese satellite. So, the Moscow line is clear. It's now up to the British.

CAMPBELL *shrugs. But has listened carefully, to something that he had not entirely expected.*

SOVIET AMBASSADOR: (*relaxing, having spent his political penny's worth*) Congratulations, by the way, Comrade Co-President. The King likes you. Did you know that? Your Embassy is now out of – what do the Americans say? – out of the 'doghouse'. Or, as you British say, 'out of Coventry'. Have I got that right? I never went there, when I was in our London Embassy. I enjoyed the London nightlife too much. Incidentally, where is Coventry? No, don't tell me. (*Pulling a bottle and two glasses out of a desk drawer*). Will you join me in a glass of vodka? Here's to the day when you and I, Comrade Chargé d'Affaires, get sent somewhere more civilised, more sympathetic. Possibly, Cuba? *Na zdorovje!*

Int. The Chancery of the US Embassy.

US CHARGÉ D'AFFAIRES: (ALF GAGE, *Harvard-educated, East Coast, 'Boston Brahmin', a little older than* CAMPBELL, *and with a natural affinity to the British. Both men relaxed.*) Well done, Bob. That's one of us out of the 'doghouse'. You must teach me how to dance 'The Twist', sometime. (*They laugh, easily and naturally*). Seriously, I know what you think. Privately, I tend to agree. I was really sorry, when Washington spiked the British Peace Plan for Cambodia.

But the fact is that, these days, the 'Crazies' are in charge, in Washington. They simply cannot wrap their minds around the idea of a neutral Cambodia, or a neutral anyone else for that matter.

ROBERT CAMPBELL: I know, I know. But what about 'Nam?

US CHARGÉ D'AFFAIRES: In my personal view, the US ought to be looking for a way out, militarily; the South Vietnamese don't really have their hearts in the fight, and if they don't, why should Uncle Sam?

ROBERT CAMPBELL: And Eisenhower's famous 'Domino Theory'? If Vietnam topples, according to some of you guys, then Cambodia, Laos, Thailand, Malaysia will all follow. One after another. Maybe even the Galapagos Islands, eventually!

US CHARGÉ D'AFFAIRES: Quite honestly, Bob, I don't rate it. Just some theory of the National Security Council, some years back. But there's not a blind thing that I can do, to help secure a neutral Cambodia, even if that were attainable.

Simply no one in Washington understands the God-King, let alone begins actually to like the guy. His 'street cred' in the Oval Office and in Foggy Bottom is now precisely nil. A pity, I grant. But nil. Zilch. *Niente!*

ROBERT CAMPBELL: (*sarcastically*)Well, thanks a million. Makes life really easy for poor old H.M.G. To say nothing of the poor old King! And, by the way, I actually like the guy, respect him too, and not only because there's no bloody alternative. The King's got more politically savvy in his little finger than your President has in his entire cerebellum! Pardon my French!

US CHARGÉ D'AFFAIRES: (*Changes tone. Grins broadly*) Yep! By the way, how *do* you Brits manage to be so very balanced and so very fair-minded? Disconcerting! Unnerving, even! Makes us feel naïve, cotton-picking, Johnny-come-latelies, on the international scene. (*Waves at a tray on a side table*). Care for a Budweiser?

ROBERT CAMPBELL: Come off it, Alf! Remember Harold Macmillan. We Brits are just Greeks in the Roman Empire.

US CHARGÉ D'AFFAIRES: Yeah. Sure. I don't think. Not that I'd noticed.

Ext. **The bar of the Foreign Correspondent's Club overlooking the Mekong river. The 'Happy Hour'.**

Crowded with boozers, mostly French businessmen, engineers and aid workers. A few local hacks. Noisy. No one pays any attention to who comes and who goes. CAMPBELL *enters, orders a Pernod, catches* LeBRUN*'s eye. They drift unnoticed, through the drunks, towards the balcony. They speak in French.*

MAURICE LeBRUN: It is not possible, I regret, Monsieur, for the two of us to remain here very long together, this evening. People will talk. Accordingly, let us be brief.

ROBERT CAMPBELL: Right, understood. So, to be blunt, M. LeBrun, what am I here for? In your view, what do I do next?

MAURICE LeBRUN: Against every political instinct, M. Campbell, I have a certain soft spot for the English. They stood firm against Hitler, when the French bourgeoisie threw in the towel. But I despise your Tory politicians, and don't think much of your Labour ones, either. I am a true Socialist. (*Campbell shrugs*).

Therefore, I shall simply say this. The only way forward, for Cambodia, is with a neutral status, but pro-Beijing and with Chinese political and military guarantees. I am desolated, but no one else and nothing else matters. Not even the Americans. They'll be out of Indo-China, with their tail between their legs, within the next three years or less. France, Russia and the rest, they do not count either.

ROBERT CAMPBELL: You paint a negative picture, M. LeBrun.

MAURICE LeBRUN: Perhaps. But my point is that, today, the key lies in your hands, M. Campbell. How should one put this, to avoid offence? We all know that, these days, your government are accustomed to kowtow to Washington. This time, I invite the English to try to be Free Men, as you were, back in 1940 – *without* the United States, I may remind you.

ROBERT CAMPBELL: What about Beijing – and Mao's followers among the Khmers?

MAURICE LeBRUN: (*looks around, lowers his voice*). In due course, I shall introduce you to Saloth Sar of the Khmer Rouge. Otherwise known as Pol Pot. He is out in the jungle as I speak, with his partisans. He desires a new Marxist heaven in Cambodia. Starting from what he sees as 'Year Zero'. But only if Beijing goes along with it.

At the moment, my influential Chinese friends tell me that Beijing is still disposed to accept a Peace Conference. My advice to you, Campbell, and to your Prime Minister, is to make a determined move, as soon as you decently can. It will be your last chance. It may well be Cambodia's last chance too! (*Raises his Pernod glass*). Santé, mon brave! (*Drains the glass, and leaves, without a backward glance*).

Ext. The banks of the Mekong river in Phnom Penh.

CAMPBELL *and* DAN McGUIRE, *Head of The Cultural Foundation, are walking alone, in the moonlight. The latter has declined to receive* CAMPBELL *in the Foundation office, for fear of their conversation being overheard, or recorded by a clandestine microphone.* McGUIRE *speaks with a slight Bronx accent. He is a rough diamond.*

ROBERT CAMPBELL: Let me level with you, Dan. I am perfectly aware that you're really 'Agency'. MI6 briefed me, before I got here. I'm a 'Dip' not a 'Spook' myself. But I have been 'cleared' up to the gills. I used to liaise with your people, when I was on the Defence desk, in London.

DAN McGUIRE: I know it. Which is why we are walking and talking here on the river bank. No need to rustle papers or run taps into a basin, while we chat, ha ha. Like in the novels.

ROBERT CAMPBELL: Splendid! So, what's the message? As you see it, here and now, on the ground?

DAN McGUIRE: Nothing much to add to what Alf had to say to you, in his office – yes, I'm in the picture on that. I agree for once with State and disagree with the 'Crazies'.

ROBERT CAMPBELL: OK. Me too. So what happens next?

DAN McGUIRE: Quite soon, now, the President will stop pussy-footing with arms supplies and military so-called 'advisers' in 'Nam. He'll commit combat troops. Send in the Marines. But Vietnam is not Korea; it simply won't work. Our guys won't be able to tell one gook from another.

ROBERT CAMPBELL: Come again? I don't quite follow you.

DAN McGUIRE: Look, in Malaya during the emergency, you Brits could do just that – the Clandestine Chinese Organisation, out in the jungle, was one thing, while your Malays were another. Hot diggedy-dog, they even looked different from each other, ethnically. There was some sort of public order. The police force functioned. The locals were on your side. They tipped you off.

ROBERT CAMPBELL: I've heard that. My Defence Attaché fought in Malaya.

DAN McGUIRE: Well now, as you will find out, Vietnam is utterly different. In the jungles and paddy fields, the 'grunts' won't have a clue who is a friend and who is an enemy. And you and I sure will know all about it, here in Cambodia. Yes, Sir!

ROBERT CAMPBELL: What do you mean by that, Dan? What are you afraid of?

DAN McGUIRE: Ignore, for the moment, the wilder US press stories of a six-lane 'Ho Chi Minh Trail' through the remoter Cambodian frontier districts. But, sooner or later, it's going to come. Cambodian landowners and traders will want to back both sides against the middle. The local authorities will turn a blind eye, even if the Vietcong decide to abuse Cambodian neutrality on a large scale. But the US President will *not* turn a blind eye.

ROBERT CAMPBELL: Dan, you make me feel really depressed. What the heck do the White House think they're up to? Can't you do something about this?

DAN McGUIRE: Mind you, Bob, that's just me, talking off the record. It's not the good old US of A talking. Nor even the 'Agency'. But I've spent years in this part of the world. It's what a mad Irishman thinks, so it is.

What do we do, you ask? Meaning, you, Bob Campbell? Well, I'll tell you. You go for it. Revive the British Peace Plan. Before it's too bloddy late, Mother of God. Too bloddy late.

Ext. The garden of the Australian Ambassador's Residence.

RANKIN *and* CAMPBELL *are seated in wicker armchairs, on a closely cut lawn. They are drinking Foster's lager, at sunset.*

ROBERT CAMPBELL: Well, there you are, Noel. That's who I've seen. That's what they said.

NOEL RANKIN: 'Struth, Bob! What's your conclusion?

ROBERT CAMPBELL: The universal message is that the Brits were on the right course, and should get back on track again, as soon as possible. I'm a bit scared to say it, but I think they're right. And that's precisely what I aim to try and bring about.

NOEL RANKIN: Plumb right, Bob. I only wish Canberra would stick their head above the parapet, too. At present, they won't – America is our protector now, not the Raj and the British Empire. But I personally will do everything possible to help.

ROBERT CAMPBELL: How, Noel, exactly? Up front? Tomorrow?

NOEL RANKIN: Beginning, strangely enough Bob, with a visit up-country, to the shrine of the "Crocodile Princess". (*Smirking, knowingly*) Why not get *Martine* to take you?

Ext. The veranda of the British Embassy's *maison flottante*.

CAMPBELL *and* MARTINE *alone, leaning on the balustrade, watching the river rush by, in the afternoon sun. They speak in*

English.

MARTINE LEFEVRE: *THE "CROCODILE PRINCESS"!* Are you absolutely *crazy*, Bob? I thought you lived in the modern world, like me.

ROBERT CAMPBELL: Nevertheless, that's what Ambassador Rankin said. He speaks the Cambodian language fluently. He knows your culture well. He has better connections at Court than I do. He must know what he's talking about.

MARTINE LEFEVRE: All this is *sheer superstition*. I know our King takes it seriously. His astrologers, too. But it makes no sense. Do me a favour! Some sub-teen Princess gets taken by a crocodile, two hundred years ago and more. Corpse ends up, intact and incorrupt, inside the now captured crocodile, miles away up river. They build her a shrine in the jungle, at the end of nowhere. Today, the King kowtows to her memory. She's supposed to protect the Kingdom. Speaks to the King through a medium. Is in touch with our Cambodian sky gods - the 'Tevodas'. Give me a break, Bob! If I smoked, I'd want a fag off you.

ROBERT CAMPBELL: I don't disagree, Martine. All wildly far-fetched, to me. But there are so many things on earth and in heaven which were not dreamed about by Descartes. And, frankly, I'm in need of help. Including *your* help.

MARTINE LEFEVRE: In need of *help* ......?

ROBERT CAMPBELL: Bob Campbell, as you well know, is a limited creature. But he will now go anywhere, talk to anyone, do anything, to try to save this innocent country of yours. There's no point in beating about the bush. Cambodia is in deep danger. You may think that I'm just a playboy of the 'Swinging Sixties'. Up to a point, perhaps I am. But I also happen to be something else.

MARTINE LEFEVRE: (*reaches out her arms, smiling*) Bob. Wonderful! You're so special! I love you. There. I've admitted it.

ROBERT CAMPBELL: (*taken by surprise; not quite grasping her sense*) And the Crocodile Princess? You'll go there, with me? Won't you? Pretty please!

MARTINE LEFEVRE: If you're nice. To me. Now. This minute.

CAMPBELL *recovers; puts his arms round* MARTINE'S *waist and kisses her.*

PART TWO: HIGH NOON

Ext. **A small Cambodian village on the banks of the Mekong river, remote from the capital.**

Wooden houses on stilts, no one about, except for CAMPBELL *and* MARTINE. *Late afternoon. Grey rain clouds overhead. They are standing in a clearing. In front of them is a Cambodian monastery with open sides. In the dark interior, at the far end, lit by candles, looms a golden image of the Buddha. Religious chants can be heard from an adjoining building, to the right. To the left, on the other side of the clearing, a conical stone tomb, erected over the ashes of the long defunct "Crocodile Princess".*

MARTINE LEFEVRE: Well, we made it, Bob. This is it.
 (*sarcastically*) The tomb at the centre of the secret beliefs of the Kings of Cambodia.
ROBERT CAMPBELL: Spooky, and then some. Why is it seemingly deserted?
MARTINE LEFEVRE: Not sure. My first visit, too. And, as far as I am concerned, my last. I never dreamt I'd ever come here. Papa, as you know, was dead against it. Foreigners never come here. Cambodians avoid it like the plague. Apart from the monks, the local community is tiny – just a few peasants and a Chinese shopkeeper. Frankly, it gives me the creeps.

ROBERT CAMPBELL: Simply marvellous of you to come – I'd never have found it. Not off the beaten track, like this. And my Cambodian, as you know, is laughable.

MARTINE LEFEVRE: Now we are here, what do you want to do? If you're going to speak to the Princess, just relax and do so in English. I'll translate into Khmer. It's up to you to make the running.

They walk across the clearing to the plinth on which the pyramid stands. It is dilapidated, cracked, moss-covered. CAMPBELL *shivers, then squares his shoulders, looks up and speaks. At each pause,* MARTINE *speaks out the Cambodian translation respectfully, in a high, clear voice.*

ROBERT CAMPBELL: (*stilted and self conscious*) Princess, I come to your tomb, not knowing who you are or how you fit in to the scheme of things in this country ...... I am a stranger from the other end of the earth, from a different religion ...... I shrink from spirits and the supernatural – I am a little afraid of them ...... But I respect the ways of others, I wish Cambodia well, and I need all the help I can enlist ...... So, today, I am here to ask for your assistance.

CAMPBELL *walks forward, ascends the lower steps around the tomb. Looks up again.*

ROBERT CAMPBELL: Princess. You know this country is in danger. It stands on the brink of war and risks destruction ......Under the Tevodas, it is you who are the Protector of Cambodia, the Counsellor of its Kings ...... Will you not help me?

He mounts a further step, but slips on the moss and nearly falls. He grimaces and carefully descends, to rejoin MARTINE.

ROBERT CAMPBELL: (*whispering to Martine*) She doesn't want me here. What do I do? We can't just leave.

She nods at the tomb and indicates that he should continue. She puts her finger to his lips, points at herself and shakes her head. Indicates that, this time, she wants CAMPBELL *to speak without interruption for translation.*

ROBERT CAMPBELL: My government's Peace Plan for Cambodia, to guarantee independence and neutrality, is in difficulty. The King is uncertain what to do; his ministers are in disarray. But it is still not too late. I pledge myself and my Government to try again. We have no selfish interest, no designs against your country, no desire to interfere where we are not welcome. Please do what you can to help me, Princess – for your own country's sake. I respectfully seek your understanding and I very much need your help.

He turns to MARTINE, *takes her arm and leads her back across the clearing.*

ROBERT CAMPBELL: Thank you. I think we should leave now. Maybe this was all a waste of time. If not superstition, then blasphemous presumption. I do *not* feel welcome.

MARTINE LEFEVRE: (*feeling unexpectedly moved*) Bob, I'm not sure about that. You spoke the truth. You meant no harm – quite the reverse. But, yes, we should leave, now.

They quit the clearing, passing through the village. An old woman with a wrinkled brown face appears from the shadows and gazes curiously at them, mumbling to herself. MARTINE *smiles and gives her alms. It starts to drizzle and the light begins to fade. They reach the banks of the river, where a pirogue is waiting for them. It will take them down river to a small town where they have parked their Land Rover. The boat swings out against the current, turns and sets course to the South.* CAMPBELL *stares moodily across at the jungle, where he picks out the pinnacle at the top of the tomb. He watches, until it passes out of sight. Sighs. Smiles in self-deprecation at* MARTINE. *They gaze at each other, unblinking, each with their own inner thoughts. Move closer. Kiss. Stay in each other's arms, in the growing darkness.*

Int. Three days later. The office of the Australian Ambassador.

CAMPBELL *and* RANKIN *are alone.*

NOEL RANKIN: Bob, don't come all coy and embarrassed. You did the right thing – and I'm *not* coming the raw prawn! What do you intend to do next?

ROBERT CAMPBELL: I need to make absolutely sure that the Cambodians are still fully on board, before I stick my neck out with London and Washington. I know what the King wants. A full Geneva Peace Conference on Cambodia, on the lines already proposed. I know what the Prime Minister, and most of the Cambodian Cabinet, want, too. The same thing, with brass knobs on. I met the Prime Minister very discreetly last night, for a one-on-one, just him and me, no sidekicks present.

NOEL RANKIN: How did you manage that?

ROBERT CAMPBELL: I met him in a private room, at his favourite opium den.

NOEL RANKIN: You mean, *Chez La Mère Chhum*? (CAMPBELL *nods*). I know it. I went there too, once. It's controlled by the Queen Mother. She's on our side. No one will say a word. Well done. So, what did he say?

ROBERT CAMPBELL: What you'd expect. Cambodia's only chance. Go for it, before the Communists change their minds. (CAMPBELL *rises to leave*). Which is why I need to do two more things. See General Lon Nol. (RANKIN *nods*). And then check with the Khmer Rouge. Guess what? Our mutual friend Maurice LeBrun says he can fix a meeting with Saloth Sar.

NOEL RANKIN: Saloth Sar? Alias Pol Pot? Watch your back. If it leaks, you'll be in deep trouble, back here. Consorting with the enemy…

ROBERT CAMPBELL: Noel, I simply *have* to. If I can tick that box too, the Brits will get back to the Yanks and the peace process can be re-launched. If the White House gives the thumbs up, the South Vietnamese, too, will scramble on board, whatever their alleged objections so far. It's time to "rock-and-roll"!

Ext. A holiday resort at Kep, on the Cambodian coast. A large luxury hotel.

GENERAL LON NOL, *a tall, well-built man, in a brightly coloured bathing robe, is relaxing under an awning, with a large glass of whisky in his hand.* CAMPBELL, *staying at the same hotel by arrangement, is seated beside him, looking out to sea. They speak French.*

GENERAL LON NOL: Yes, it's still OK by me. But it's the very last time. Me, I'd rather Cambodia was in full alliance with the US. I don't trust the Chinese. I detest the Vietnamese. I don't much like the way the King does whatever Beijing tells him. But a neutral Cambodia, OK, if that's what the *Americans* really want.

ROBERT CAMPBELL: I think what *they* really want is to settle the war in Vietnam. And then, go. A genuinely neutral Cambodia would be one less thing for Uncle Sam to worry about. But they don't want to de-moralise the South Vietnamese.

GENERAL LON NOL: De-moralise the South Vietnamese? You're joking, Monsieur Campbell.

ROBERT CAMPBELL: *You* know, General ...... not encourage the Viets in Saigon to think that they can go neutral, too.

GENERAL LON NOL: To Hell with the Vietnamese. They're all the same, Viet Cong and anti-Viet Cong, North and South, and the rest. They think they're smarter than us Cambodians. They'd like to enslave us and grab our territory. If I had my way, instead of letting the Viets keep settling in dribs and drabs in Cambodia, I'd expel the whole lot. (*Laughs uproariously.*) Who needs them? Not us Cambodians. No, Sir. The French used to have the right idea. You know their expression: *"Pas de complexe. Il faut casser du Viet"!* Cheers, Monsieur Campbell!

Ext. Angkor. In front of Angkor Thom. Evening.

The Royal Ballet, led by PRINCESS DEVI SRI *as prima ballerina, are performing on a floodlit stage, to oriental music from the orchestra of the Royal Court, with the temple as backdrop.* THE KING *has invited foreign Heads of Mission and other dignitaries up to Angkor. They are seated in several rows of plush chairs,* THE KING *at the centre front. Behind them, the Auberge des Temples, a new luxury tourist hotel, has been taken over for the occasion; a sumptuous buffet can be seen through the open plate glass doors, awaiting the guests after the performance.*

During the interval in the programme, LeBRUN *sidles up to* CAMPBELL *through the throng. He speaks quietly, looking away in the opposite direction, to avoid attention. Conversation is in French.*

MAURICE LeBRUN: M. Campbell, I have arranged for you to encounter Saloth Sar. His base to the North is not so far away. The rendezvous will be at the edge of the temple complex. Difficult to find. I propose to conduct you there, myself.

ROBERT CAMPBELL: (*in English to the passing Japanese Ambassador, in order to distract attention from* LeBRUN) A fine spectacle, Excellency, the 'Flower Blessing Dance'. But I'm dying for my supper! (THE AMBASSADOR *smiles, bows, and passes on.* CAMPBELL *looks over* LeBRUN'S *shoulder*). When? What time?

MAURICE LeBRUN: We shall set off at five tomorrow evening. From the hotel, on foot. It will consume half an hour to get there. The King and his entourage – and their police escort – will have left by then. No one much will be around, except a few tourists – and they will not leave the beaten path. You understand me?

ROBERT CAMPBELL: Sorry, but I'll need to bring Martine Lefèvre as my interpreter, in case he insists on going all proletarian, and speaking Khmer.

MAURICE LeBRUN: If you insist. She is, after all, a socialist, of a sort. But she must be sworn to secrecy. Also, tell her to dress down. Saloth Sar despises the bourgeoisie. He has reason. So do I!

ROBERT CAMPBELL: OK. And I'll be ultra-discreet. If asked, I'll say I'm staying on for a couple of days holiday, with Martine.

(LeBRUN *shrugs, and moves off through the crowd*).

Ext. The Banteay Chhmar Temple on the outskirts of the Angkor Wat complex. Towards sunset.

CAMPBELL, MARTINE *and* LeBRUN *are standing alone. Listening. They are simply dressed* – MARTINE *in jeans and dark blue, open-*

necked shirt. They have reached the temple along a narrow footpath through the tropical forest. The ruins are covered in creepers, fenced in by trees. Suddenly, the monkeys in the immediately surrounding jungle fall silent.

Out of the trees steps the Cambodian revolutionary leader, SALOTH SAR, *with his deputy,* KANG KEK IEU *and a* BODYGUARD. *The three are dressed identically in black, peasant, clothes, with red scarves round their necks. The guard carries a panga and stares menacingly.* SALOTH SAR *(revolutionary name 'Pol Pot') is a stocky, short man in his 'forties, already running to fat. He has an authoritative air; something manic, also. He speaks French well, but with a deliberately proletarian accent, having spent much time with the Far Left, in the Paris industrial suburbs, while on a training scheme to qualify as a primary school teacher.* KANG KEK IEU *('Comrade Deuch', in the later Tuol Sleng interrogation centre in Phnom Penh) is lean, with prominent ears and sly, indirect gaze.* SALOTH SAR *greets* LeBRUN *fraternally. Shakes hands much more formally with* CAMPBELL. KANG KEK IEU *does likewise, but awkwardly, as if unaccustomed to Western politesse. They both ignore* MARTINE. THE BODYGUARD, *of exceptional ugliness, glares suspiciously throughout, fingering his panga, his eyes moving from one to the other.*

SALOTH SAR/POL POT: I cannot stay long, Comrade. I will speak French. It is the Language of Revolution. (*Turning to* CAMPBELL). Monsieur, what is your question?

ROBERT CAMPBELL: It is about the Geneva Conference on Cambodia. The King and almost everyone else here seem to want it. Perhaps it can now be reactivated. Cambodia, independent, non-aligned and with full territorial integrity. The Chinese can live with that. But what about you?

SALOTH SAR/POL POT: (*reluctant to answer directly*) My ambition is that, one day, King or no King, Cambodia should be a truly socialist state. A Marxist, Maoist Cambodia. To be built from scratch, if need be, on totally new, revolutionary foundations. No bourgeois family structures. No religion. No capitalist devices, like currencies and banks. No central government. Just people power. Just the proletariat, unshackled and united.

KANG KEK IEU/COMRADE DEUCH: (*perking up, in less educated French*) And we shall start from 'Year Zero'. From the bottom up, and from the top down.

ROBERT CAMPBELL: How do you hope to bring this about? With help from the Vietcong?

SALOTH SAR/POL POT: This is something for the Cambodians to sort out among themselves. Self-determination. The will of the people. No outside interference. Not from the American Imperialists. Not from Ho Chi Minh either. Our biggest enemy, after the Yankee imperialists, are the Vietnamese. The contemptible Lon Nol and I can agree at least on that. The South Vietnamese are pathetic – but they will be defeated. The big question is what happens then. Ho Chi Minh wants to conquer Cambodia, kill the Cambodians, incorporate our territory in a Greater Vietnam.

MAURICE LeBRUN: I won't comment on that. But, logically, Comrade, a peace conference will keep the Vietnamese out, allow Cambodians to be Cambodians. The English and the

Russians want that. The peace conference is the way to achieve it. Are you for or against?

SALOTH SAR/POL POT: (*turning to* CAMPBELL *with evident reluctance*) Tell your government that we agree, as long as the conference is in accordance with the wishes of Chairman Mao Tse-tung. For us Khmer Rouge, no one else matters.

KANG KEK IEU/COMRADE DEUCH: Nothing. Chairman Mao is our sole guide, our father.

ROBERT CAMPBELL: (*blank faced*) I hear you, Comrade Pol Pot. Comrade Deuch.

SALOTH SAR *and* KANG KEK IEU *shake hands again with* CAMPBELL, *give* LeBRUN *a clenched fist salute, ignore* MARTINE, *turn and disappear into the twilight, with their ill-favoured escort.*

LeBRUN *shrugs, looking embarrassed.*

LeBRUN: *(whispers)* A true socialist. But I hypothesise that he is not quite right in the head.

LeBRUN, CAMPBELL *and* MARTINE *(who is now ashen and beginning to tremble) move off in the opposite direction, towards the nearest road, hurrying to make the most of the fading light.*

Int. The garden of General Lefè vreš villa in Phnom Penh, three days later.

MARTINE, GENERAL LEFEVRE *and* CAMPBELL *are seated in wicker* chairs, heads together, talking seriously. *This time, the conversation is in English, which the General speaks well, with a charming accent.*

ROBERT CAMPBELL: General, everything I've told you is strictly off the record. Not only about Pol Pot, but about the Prime Minister and the rest. In fact, not a word to anyone about anything – not even to your Ambassador, please! Just for the time being. (THE GENERAL *nods, reluctantly*).

MARTINE LEFEVRE: (*striking an awkward note, from emotion and mixed feelings*) Absolutely brilliant. Only a Scottish 'Aristo' could have pulled that off – weren't you at Eton and Oxford, or something?

ROBERT CAMPBELL: Fettes and Cambridge, actually! Sorry to disappoint! 'Aristo'? Piffle! My father is just a small landowner. Sorry to disappoint! Really rather undistinguished.

MARTINE LEFEVRE: Well, a Scottish 'Toff', then? Look at your flashy signet ring!

ROBERT CAMPBELL: (*irritated*) Boring, Martine! *Boring!*

MARTINE LEFEVRE: (*becomes embarrassed, glancing at her father. Tries to lighten the tone, show less tension*). Sorry, sorry.

GENERAL LEFEVRE: I should think so, too! We're socialists, dear, remember?

MARTINE LEFEVRE: I said sorry, and I meant it. It was silly of me. And yes, I *am* a socialist. In the sense of being 'pro' the people. The King is, too. That's why I support him. I'm a patriot. I love all who love him – especially the peasants in the countryside and villages. They need a leader who really cares for them. I know you feel the same way, Bob.

ROBERT CAMPBELL: Of course I do, Martine. I, too, am a 'King's Man', in that sense.

GENERAL LEFEVRE: (*impatient, and perfectly aware of* CAMPBELL*'s developing relationship with his daughter, of which he approves*) *Bon! Très bien!* Now you've got your answers, what happens next?

ROBERT CAMPBELL: London have called me back for consultations. Off tomorrow. Flying East – I'm instructed to pop into Washington first.

MARTINE LEFEVRE: God go with you. The Crocodile Princess, too, for that matter! I shan't rest till you're returned. What is your Scottish expression? "Haste ye back!". Old Mrs McDowell taught us that, when I was at the Monkey Club in London, acquiring a ...... social 'polish' ...... at Daddy's vast expense.

ROBERT CAMPBELL: Martine, General, don't let's count our chickens before they're hatched. We have another expression up in the Highlands. "There's aye a muckle slappy steen, at ilka body's door".

MARTINE LEFEVRE: Excuse me?

ROBERT CAMPBELL Oh, sorry. Let me translate. "There's always a slippery stone at everybody's door".

GENERAL LEFEVRE: Yes. Too damned true, Campbell. Especially in today's Cambodia!

Interlude. Scenes without dialogue.

Silent Pictures of CAMPBELL *in the State Department in*

Washington, and the West Wing of The White House, with an Embassy colleague, cajoling senior officials and lobbying personal friends. Then, in the Foreign Secretary's Office in London, and over to Number 10 Downing Street, to see the Private Secretary. Nods all round. Shots of the Prime Minister (Harold Wilson) on the Hot Line to President Johnson.

CAMPBELL *flies back to Phnom Penh. He calls on the US Chargé d'Affaires, and the Australian and French Ambassadors, who listen carefully and then shake hands in congratulation. The same at* GENERAL LEFEVRE *'s villa.* MARTINE *embraces* CAMPBELL, *warmly. The* GENERAL *opens some champagne. At Madam Chhum's opium den,* PRINCE MONIVONG, *the Cambodian Prime Minister, rises gravely from his couch, and shakes* CAMPBELL'S *hand also.*

PART THREE: BOLT FROM A BLUE SKY

Ext. The Foreign Correspondent's Club, Phnom Penh, the following evening.

On the balcony overlooking the river, CAMPBELL *and* LeBRUN *are standing by themselves, watching the sunset. Conversation in French.*

MAURICE LeBRUN: I do not well know how to express this, M. Campbell. But Beijing has just performed a *volte-face*. Me, I'm appalled! But the Chinese Government have just decided to block the British initiative for a Geneva Peace Conference on Cambodia. They are not prepared to attend; nor will the North Vietnamese.

ROBERT CAMPBELL: Block? You must be joking!

MAURICE LeBRUN: I regret, but I am far from making a pleasantry. Indeed, I confess I now find myself distinctly apprehensive.

ROBERT CAMPBELL: Why?

MAURICE LeBRUN: Because this change of policy emanates from the very top. From Chairman Mao Tse-tung himself. He is angry at the military escalation in South Vietnam; the day and night bombing of the North.

ROBERT CAMPBELL: How do you know this?

MAURICE LeBRUN: I come from last week's Asian Conference in Indonesia. I returned only yesterday. The Chinese asked for a side meeting with the King, Comrade Chou En-lai told His

Majesty that a Geneva Conference was no longer admissible. The Americans intended to dupe Cambodia, aiming to use the Peace Conference on Cambodia to start side talks about a settlement in Vietnam. But Beijing was not prepared to negotiate, over Vietnam. The Americans must withdraw at once or suffer defeat and humiliation.

ROBERT CAMPBELL: And the King's reaction?

MAURICE LeBRUN: Naturally, shocked to the core. He has been calling for this Peace Conference for some time. It's an extremely bitter pill. Nevertheless, the message coming from Chou and therefore Mao personally, His Majesty felt he had no choice but to fall in line. I know what an effort you have undertaken, M. Campbell. But it is now – how might you English put it? – a totally new playing field.

Anyway – you must admit – Cambodia is just a sideshow, for Washington and Beijing alike. The only thing that seems to matter, at the moment, is the Vietnam War. In my view, this can now only escalate. That's why I am so apprehensive. Quite soon, Cambodia will get dragged under.

ROBERT CAMPBELL: What am I going to tell London? Our Foreign Secretary will be here, early next week, to tell the King that, at long last, he's now got his Peace Conference!

MAURICE LeBRUN: No self-flagellation, M. Campbell. It is not your fault. It was unpredictable. The King will speak on national radio, tonight. I have seen the first draft of what he proposes to say. It is, of course, totally negative – a complete U turn, in established Cambodian Foreign Policy.

By the way, the King tells me he will not receive your

Foreign Minister. His Majesty has a pressing prior engagement, up-country. You will have to make do with seeing a member of the Cambodian Cabinet.

ROBERT CAMPBELL: I can hardly wrap my mind around this. Are you dead certain? Should I ask to see the King himself, before my Minister hits town?

MAURICE LeBRUN: The King thinks you *très sage*. By all means ask for an Audience. But me, I will have to keep out of it – His Majesty is, I hope, unaware that we are meeting like this. Ask through normal Cambodian channels, if you please.

ROBERT CAMPBELL: What about my Foreign Secretary, though?

MAURICE LeBRUN: Permit me to repeat. The King simply will not receive him. Meanwhile, I suggest that you watch out for fireworks. The street mob are going to be let loose again. Not against you English, this time, but against the US Embassy. It is timed to coincide with your Minister's visit, just to reinforce the King's message.

ROBERT CAMPBELL: Oh my God. Not again!

MAURICE LeBRUN: There is something further, if I might be permitted to add? The King will shortly break off diplomatic relations altogether with the US, and expel the US Embassy. Just to prove to China that, even though theoretically neutral, the King remains a true friend of Chairman Mao Tse-tung.

CAMPBELL *shakes his head, in disbelief. A club waiter approaches, and is waved away.* CAMPBELL *leaves, white-faced, while* LeBRUN *stares moodily across the Mekong, alone with his thoughts, as night begins to fall.*

Int. The British Embassy.

CAMPBELL *in his office, the following morning, dictating to his* SECRETARY. *He speaks deliberately and slowly, with pauses to find the right words.*

ROBERT CAMPBELL: Cipher telegram to London, Barbara, please. Classification: Confidential. Flash Priority: Most Urgent. Following Personal for Secretary of State, from Chargé d'Affaires, Phnom Penh. Copied to HM Ambassador, Washington and HM Chargé d'Affaires, Beijing. Text begins:

Paragraph 1. There has been a major and entirely unexpected shift in Cambodian Foreign Policy, which affects everything decided in London and Washington last week.

Paragraph 2. Last night, the King announced, in a major speech in Phnom Penh, that he no longer wished the convening of a Geneva Peace Conference, to guarantee this country's neutrality.

Paragraph 3. I have just returned from a private audience with the King. He confirmed his position. He has no objection to your visit to Phnom Penh next week, but much regrets he will not be able to receive you. He will be "out of town"!

[Flashback to earlier in the morning.

The King's Private Palace. CAMPBELL *is speaking quietly in French.* THE KING — *a diminutive Oriental figure in Western dress, dark suit, white shirt — sits on the edge of his chair. Interrupts* CAMPBELL, *shakes his head, giggles nervously, indicates that the audience is at an end.*]

ROBERT CAMPBELL: Paragraph 4. This extraordinary shift follows the King's meeting with Prime Minister Chou En-lai in Jakarta at the end of last week. According to a close Royal Advisor who was present, the Chinese warned the King that belated US agreement to a Geneva Conference was, in reality, a trap.

Paragraph 5. I recommend that you maintain the schedule for Cambodia next week. I have the agreement of the Foreign Minister to receive you. The Cambodian Prime Minister, too, if you wish.

Text ends.

Thank you, Barbara. As soon as you can, please. I'll need to cast a last eye over the draft, before transmission. I've alerted everyone. We must get this telegram off, within the hour.

Ext. The veranda of the British Embassy's *maison flottante*. The following day.

CAMPBELL, *his* SECRETARY *and* McGUIRE *are preparing to go out water-skiing. They are all in swimming clothes and lifejackets; but* McGUIRE *also sports his characteristic bowler hat and chomps on a long cigar. The* CAMBODIAN CARETAKER *of the houseboat, his ears flapping, is in the background.* McGUIRE *takes* CAMPBELL *by the elbow and walks him to the corner of the balustrade, speaks out of the corner of his mouth into* CAMPBELL*'s ear.*

DAN McGUIRE: I can't talk here, Bob, but something 'mega' is happening. You need to know. It's extremely sensitive. I'll be able to talk more freely, when we are out on the water.

(CAMPBELL *nods, but says nothing*).

Ext. In the middle of the river Mekong.

CAMPBELL *and* McGUIRE *are both waterskiing, being towed behind the Embassy launch steered by Campbell's secretary,* BARBARA. *The two men converge to speak, side-by-side.*

DAN McGUIRE: Great to talk, Bob. But don't report this through your channels. Simply too sensitive. Our London Head of Station is briefing your Foreign Secretary, at this minute.

ROBERT CAMPBELL: (*a trifle impatiently*) Spit it out, Dan, for Pete's sake! What the Hell is all this about?

DAN McGUIRE: Here we go. Massive change in pattern of Vietcong clandestine activity, on Cambodian soil. The 'Ho Chi Minh Trail' is finally here. For real.

ROBERT CAMPBELL: But we've checked this out before, Dan. The trail is a myth, dear to right-wing journalists and some of your generals in Saigon.

DAN McGUIRE: No longer. Satellite photography. Intercepts. Three absolutely reliable local agents, up-country. Checked out by our Special Forces, with their own eyes.

ROBERT CAMPBELL: Meaning what, precisely?

DAN McGUIRE: New fuel and ammo dumps. New staging camps in the jungle. Very considerable movement – mostly coolies on foot, but also large numbers of 'Charlie Cong' on bicycles.

ROBERT CAMPBELL: Level with me, Dan. Is all this truly, truly for real? Or just invented evidence, for some devious purpose of the Pentagon?

DAN McGUIRE: The former, Bob. 'Fraid so. Your intelligence people in Washington have seen the raw evidence. The war is now coming to Cambodia. Finally. And what a goddamn shame!

ROBERT CAMPBELL: You can say that again.

DAN McGUIRE: One last thing. It's goodbye, Bob. I'm being expelled from Cambodia, so I am! Forty-eight hours notice to pack up and go. Flying out tomorrow afternoon. I've been declared *persona non grata*. But that isn't all ......

ROBERT CAMPBELL: Tell me.

DAN McGUIRE: My own agents confirm what Maurice LeBrun hinted to you yesterday. The King really does intend to break off relations with the US. Not a single one of his key ministers and advisors want anything of the kind. But, it's coming, any day now.

McGUIRE *throws the stub of his cigar into the water, spits and doffs his bowler hat.* CAMPBELL *shouts to his secretary to pick up speed.* CAMPBELL *and* McGUIRE *race off, veering away from each other, weaving in and out.*

Int. The Office of the Cambodian Foreign Minister, the following week. Scene without words.

The BRITISH FOREIGN SECRETARY *(accompanied by* CAMPBELL, *plus a* PRIVATE SECRETARY *from London) is engaged in an* animated discussion with his opposite number. *Pauses, in which the two men stare at each other.* The CAMBODIAN FOREIGN MINISTER *is uncomfortable in the extreme; deflects his gaze; shrugs.* CAMPBELL *intervenes. Similar reaction. Finally, on a sign from* CAMPBELL, *the British rise and take their leave.*

Ext. Outside the Cambodian Foreign Ministry.

The three British prepare to climb into CAMPBELL*'s large black Austin Princess, flag fluttering on the bonnet, door held open by a flunky. A noise makes everyone freeze – the roar of a street mob, in the distance; raucous loud speakers; blare of martial music.*

ROBERT CAMPBELL: I'm afraid it's started, Secretary of State. The target is the US Embassy. We'd better get back to our own Chancery, immediately.

FOREIGN SECRETARY *nods; they head off onto the main boulevard.*

Int. The British Embassy Chancery.

CAMPBELL *and his senior embassy staff; the* FOREIGN SECRETARY *and his* PRIVATE SECRETARY.

FOREIGN SECRETARY: We really must visit the scene of the attack, don't you think? Show solidarity with the Americans. Reason with the crowd. Get the police to pull the rioters back.

ROBERT CAMPBELL: Interesting idea, Sir. But it won't work. Or not yet. These demonstrations are normally tightly controlled. They have a beginning, a middle and an end. It's a question, not of *whether* we go, but *when*.

FOREIGN SECRETARY: What do you suggest, Campbell?

ROBERT CAMPBELL: I suggest we divide our forces, in the following way. Secretary of State, you go with the Vice-Consul, to call on the Dean of the Diplomatic Corps. Tell him what is afoot. Try to persuade him to intervene with the authorities. It's his duty to do this – even if he's Russian, foxy and KGB.

I'll remove my jacket and tie, slide off in an unmarked car and recce the riot. I know my way around the back streets. I won't stick my neck out too far. But we need to know exactly what's happening.

The Military Attaché here will stay and guard the fort. I should like everything locked up; non-essential staff sent home; official transport moved out. Just in case. OK Colonel?

MILITARY ATTACHÉ: Fine, Bob.

PRIVATE SECRETARY: Then what?

ROBERT CAMPBELL: (*to the* SECRETARY OF STATE) You, Sir, the Private Secretary and I meet back here. Then move off towards the US Embassy. No jackets, no ties, my unmarked private car. Nothing conspicuous. We take a close look. Do what we can. Just one thing, though.

FOREIGN SECRETARY: (*slightly huffy*) Which is what, if you please Campbell?

ROBERT CAMPBELL: I've been through all this before, with rioters. So have the Colonel and the rest of us. The Phnom Penh street mob is not nice. It's capable of getting just a little bit over-excited. Liable to exceed its instructions. (THE COLONEL *and the* VICE-CONSUL *nod their heads*). Therefore, please be precisely guided by me, Sir, in what we do and how we do it.

MILITARY ATTACHÉ: He's absolutely right, Sir, I'm afraid.

FOREIGN SECRETARY: (*resigned*) If you and Campbell say so, Colonel.

Ext. Street scene near the US Embassy.

The three Brits are in a side road, trying to get a clear view of the US Embassy, seen in the middle distance – stones flying, rioters hammering on the metal doors and window shutters. The three men sidle forward, get jostled, start attracting attention. Surprised glances from the rioters; then black looks; then hoarse voices and pointing fingers. THE PRIVATE SECRETARY *gets shoved in the ribs.* CAMPBELL *is spat upon. He signals a withdrawal. They edge back down the street; come to a sleazy bar.* CAMPBELL *opens the door, to bundle them all in. But, before he does so:*

ROBERT CAMPBELL: We tell them we are Norwegian seaman. Bridge officers from the "Oslo", currently in the commercial dock. Not British, *Norwegians*, got it?

FOREIGN SECRETARY: Seamen. From the "Oslo". Norwegian.

ROBERT CAMPBELL: In we go.

Int. Dingy interior of the bar.

Characters as above. Two customers in a corner, sozzled and incurious. A PRETTY BARGIRL *looks at them, eyebrows raised.* A BARMAN *in the background, with five o'clock stubble, scowls.*

ROBERT CAMPBELL: (*in French*) Good afternoon. Three beers, please. We are Norwegians. From our ship, the "Oslo". In need of refreshment, before we sail.

THE BARGIRL *serves the beer.* THE BARMAN *looks non-committal, starts polishing some glasses, but watching the party closely. The Brits start talking to each other, in cod-Norwegian, for the barman to hear.*

ROBERT CAMPBELL: *'God dag. Hoora for den Norske Fiske'!*
FOREIGN SECRETARY: *'God dag! Ja! Ik bin enkapteinen van der "Oslo"!*
PRIVATE SECRETARY: *'Hvordan har De det? Et stort glass mørkt øl. Skål!'*
ROBERT CAMPBELL: *'Ja-Ha'!*
FOREIGN SECRETARY: *'Ja'!*

Pause, while the three men stare thoughtfully into their beer glasses. CAMPBELL *turns to the barman.*

ROBERT CAMPBELL: *'Snakker De fransk? Hvor er toalettet?'*

THE BARMAN *shakes his head, uncomprehending.* THE PRIVATE SECRETARY *starts to giggle. The* FOREIGN SECRETARY *begins to look amused. The* BARMAN *looks unconvinced. Retires to a back room. From the street, the roar of the crowd abates.* CAMPBELL *looks outside. Comes back, pays the bill, with a hefty tip to* THE PRETTY BARGIRL, *who simpers.* CAMPBELL *beckons the others out onto the street.*

Ext. The street outside the bar.

The crowd are beginning to thin out, the police to become more numerous. The rioters are being shepherded away. The three Brits approach the crossroads, opposite the US Embassy front door. CAMPBELL *pops into another bar, to make a phone call. Miraculously, an American voice from inside the Embassy answers.* CAMPBELL *goes back outside, speaks in the* FOREIGN SECRETARY*'s ear. As the crowd finally disperses, US Marines in full battle dress open the door and the American Embassy Number Two beckons the Brits inside.*

Int. The US Embassy, the US Chargé d'Affaires' office on the first floor.

US CHARGÉ D'AFFAIRES: Welcome, to our humble headquarters.

(*Lop-sided grin*). Sorry about the mess. I'm just about to look at the damage. Care to come round with me? Mind where you step.

The party move around the offices, the floors of which are strewn with broken glass, stones, rotten vegetables, etc. Much shaking of hands, slightly contrived laughter, slapping of backs.

Int. The dining room of the British Residence.

CAMPBELL *and the* TWO VISITORS FROM LONDON; *the* MILITARY ATTACHÉ; *the* GERMAN, FRENCH AND AUSTRALIAN AMBASSADORS; *the* US CHARGÉ D'AFFAIRES. *The close of an informal, working dinner.*

ROBERT CAMPBELL: Secretary of State, no speech from me, your host. But, with your permission, I should like to propose a toast. (*The company rise*). Two toasts, in fact. First: Her Majesty The Queen. (THE FOREIGN SECRETARY *repeats the toast;* THE MILITARY ATTACHÉ *adds "God Bless Her!"; they all raise their glasses and drink*). Second, a double toast – to Uncle Sam and Alf Gage! (*Still standing, the others repeat the toast, reach out to clink glasses with their US colleague. Smiles all round*).

THE US CHARGÉ D'AFFAIRES: (*remaining on his feet*) Secretary of State, Mr Campbell, gentlemen. No speech from me either. And I must slip away now, to re-join my hard-pressed staff. As you already all know, the King has decided to break off relations with Washington. Frankly, I shan't be sorry to leave. But I'm sad. It's a new ball game, now, in this neck of the woods. *Hard* ball – courtesy of Uncle Ho and Chairman Mao. (*A little overcome, with a lump in his throat.*) Meanwhile, here's to everyone present. Thanks for everything. As colleagues and friends, I shall miss you all. And I shall continue to follow *your* misdeeds, Bob, for sure!

Int. The same, half an hour later.

All the non-British guests have left, except the Australian.

ROBERT CAMPBELL: (*crest-fallen, to the* FOREIGN SECRETARY) Secretary of State, I got this wrong. I know the King is supposed to be volatile and unpredictable, but ...... I've dragged you out here for no purpose and the PM will have been made to look silly, in the Oval Office.

PRIVATE SECRETARY: Come off it, Bob. (*Turning to the Foreign Secretary*). He's not being fair to himself, Sir. It's clear that there has been a major and sudden shift in the policy of the Chinese Communists. Remember those news agency reports we were looking at, this morning? Street demonstrations in Beijing, by the so-called 'Red Guards', waving the 'little red book'. Whoever they may be, you can be sure that they're doing Mao Tse-tung's bidding. Something about a 'Cultural Revolution'?

FOREIGN SECRETARY: Campbell, relax. There's absolutely no loss of face involved, for the PM. President Johnson is no chicken. He knew perfectly well what he was doing. Went along with the initiative, with his eyes open. Between ourselves, the President had been hoping to cover his back, in case Vietnam proved a no-win commitment. (*Turning to the Australian*). What do you think, Ambassador? You have been here longer than anyone. You even speak the language, isn't that right?

NOEL RANKIN: I agree, first of all, about Bob. He has done a wonderful job. About Beijing, I agree with your Private Secretary. There *has* been a seismic shift. (*Pauses, choosing his words carefully.*) But there's more to say. Speaking as an Australian, what I simply want to say, is "Thank you". Thanks for coming, Sir. Thank you for all your Government have done. Just what we dim colonials look to, from Britain. To see the big picture and give a lead. Unfortunately, due to overlong hesitation by the Yanks, it has all come a little bit too late. I can see bad times ahead, for the Cambodians. (*Lowers his voice.*) A tragedy, because they have done no harm to anyone and really don't deserve it.

PART FOUR: THE FADING OF THE LIGHT

Ext. The British Embassy maison flottante, three days on, late afternoon.

CAMPBELL *and* MARTINE, *alone, holding hands, watching the sun sink. The Mekong glitters. The palm trees on the far bank are bathed in a golden light.*

MARTINE LEFEVRE: Bob, my dearest. It is really not your fault. You've done so much, to help my country – my people.

ROBERT CAMPBELL: Kind of you. I know what you're trying to say. But ...... (*worried by something which he finds it hard to put his finger on*). You place the emphasis on *my* country, *my* people. I can understand that. But there are other countries. The world will somehow go on. You're half French, after all. Part English-educated. Western in outlook. You're a citizen of the world. One of *us*.

MARTINE LEFEVRE: But I'm half Cambodian, too, Bob. There have been times, recently, when I've felt that I'm really Cambodian through and through. I love Daddy. I love you. But I'm also *me*. I felt it, even with Saloth Sar. A dangerous man, mad even – but also in his way a patriot.

ROBERT CAMPBELL: Never mind about Pol Pot. A nutter and up to no good, in my view. It's us, I'm talking about. I don't have any problem. I love you for being *you*; for putting up with my funny British ways; for being Cambodian as well as French. By the way, I may be British, but I'm really Anglo-Scottish. My mother is English. So, I'm mixed blood, too. Anyway, you're *perfect*, is what you are.

MARTINE LEFEVRE: (*disengaging and walking along the balustrade*) You say that. But I'm still worried. Perhaps even afraid. I sense that something is going seriously wrong. Something ugly. Something under the surface. I fear for my King. I fear for Cambodia's future.

ROBERT CAMPBELL: Do you want me to see him again – the King, I mean? Now that the dust has settled. Ask him how he sees the future?

MARTINE LEFEVRE: The King? Yes, of course. But first see the PM. And see Lon Nol – start with him, in fact. Bob, please do this. Just for me. Perhaps it's being silly but ...... Maybe we could even go and see the Crocodile Princess again? Just the two of us. Whenever you can get away. Daddy will let me go, I know.

ROBERT CAMPBELL: I'm not sure about the Princess. It's your religion, not mine. She seemed to resent me, last time. I'd have to think about it. Maybe I'll see her again, one day. But not immediately. (MARTINE *nods, sadly. There is a short silence, until* CAMPBELL *resumes*). About your father. He's so possessive, so strict.

MARTINE LEFEVRE: Bob, you've got him wrong. He wants you to .... be around in our life. Wants you for a son-in-law, in fact. He more or less said so, last night.

ROBERT CAMPBELL: Now I'm *really* scared. Let's have some more champagne. Where's the bottle? Then go somewhere more private.

MARTINE LEFEVRE: (*laughing*) Stop teasing, Bob. Remember what

they've told you, about French girls. Smouldering. Susceptible.
Oo La La! That sort of thing?

ROBERT CAMPBELL: I thought you were half Cambodian.

MARTINE LEFEVRE: Just makes it worse. Passionate, oriental. No hang ups. All for it!

ROBERT CAMPBELL: OK. Let's skip the champagne bit. (*Picks her up and carries her off into the cabin*).

Int. General Lon Nol's office.

CAMPBELL *enters, shakes hands.* THE GENERAL *dismisses his ADC, pours two whiskies and sits down with* CAMPBELL. *Conversation in French.*

GENERAL LON NOL: I know why you've come. You're worried about the failure of the Peace Plan. Well, I'm only a simple soldier, but I'm not worried in the least. And I'm not alone, hereabouts. (CAMPBELL *looks puzzled*). It's time it all stopped. All this kowtowing to Beijing, turning a blind eye to the Vietcong.

ROBERT CAMPBELL: I don't like the Communists either. I was briefly involved in the Korean War. When last in London, I served on the NATO desk. But that's the *British* scene. *Cambodia's* in a different position. Surely, it has to be best for you, to stay neutral?

GENERAL LON NOL: *Real* neutrality, maybe. But not one-sided. I want diplomatic relations with the US restored. I want US military equipment; American advisors; combat troops too, if need be.

ROBERT CAMPBELL: But you won't get them. Washington won't want to get bogged down even further than they are now.

GENERAL LON NOL: Look, my friend. I want the US to win in Vietnam. I want the Viets out of Cambodia. At present, I'm not allowed to move against the Vietcong bases springing up along our frontier, on Cambodian soil. If I had my way, I'd get the Cambodian army – with or without US ground forces – to push them out. And why stop there? Why do we tolerate all these Vietnamese immigrants, in our country? They're trying to colonise us, by stealth. I'd kick them all out – by force if need be. Bye, bye, Viets!

ROBERT CAMPBELL: Cambodia for the Cambodians?

GENERAL LON NOL: I'll drink to that, Mr Chargé d'Affaires. *Il faut casser du Viet, n'est-ce pas? Santé!!*

Ext. Outside Mè re Chhum's opium den, late at night.

A low wooden house in a quiet street at the edge of Phnom Penh, standing back from the road and screened by small trees bearing blossoms. A dim light from a street lamp. Several VIP limousines parked along the pavement, their drivers snoring. Two gendarmes patrol in the distance. CAMPBELL, *in tuxedo, coming directly from a dinner party at the French Embassy, parks his sports car some way off, quietly strolls up to the entrance, mounts the steps to the veranda and is greeted by* MME CHHUM, *an elderly and much respected 'Grande Dame', whose finger tips he kisses. She smiles (she knows and likes* CAMPBELL*).*

Int. Mè re Chhumŝ opium den, late at night, lit discreetly by spirit lamps.

A youthful VIETNAMESE COURTESAN *(of striking figure and good looks, dressed in a tight-fitting silk Ao-Dai, with slits up the sides) escorts* CAMPBELL *to a changing room, where he leaves his DJ and puts on a sarong. He is then shown into the room next door, where His Highness* PRINCE MONIVONG, *the Prime Minister, is reclining on his couch. An* ANCIENT CRONE *lies on the straw matting floor beside him, preparing his opium pipe over a small burner. Her lined face in turn lit up and in shadow, as she blows on the charcoal.* PRINCE MONIVONG *shakes hands with* CAMPBELL, *and waves at a tray of drinks.* CAMPBELL *sits down opposite and begins sipping a beer.*

PRINCE MONIVONG: I know why you are here, Excellency. You are worried by the failure of the peace initiative.

ROBERT CAMPBELL: Your Highness, it is not only that. I feel uneasy. It is hard to pin down. But the atmosphere in the country is strange; feelings are unsettled.

PRINCE MONIVONG: You are well informed.

ROBERT CAMPBELL: How does Your Highness see the future?

PRINCE MONIVONG: (*trying to shift the discussion back to safer ground*) I can understand China's unwillingness to sit down at the same table as the US. The Americans are now bombing China's ally, North Vietnam, by day and night. US combat troops are committed in large numbers in the South. There is the US 'Secret War' in Laos.

ROBERT CAMPBELL: But it goes deeper than that. Mao Tse-tung has decided to write a new chapter in the history of Communism. To move to something purer, perhaps, as he sees it. But more radical and more violent. How might this impact on Cambodia?

PRINCE MONIVONG: (*evasive*) This week, I have seen the Chinese Ambassador wearing black pyjamas and accompanied by 'minders' from his junior staff – Red Guards in fact.

ROBERT CAMPBELL: But what of the future, Your Highness? Surely, great change is in the air, within Cambodia. The situation is precarious. Great dangers surround you.

PRINCE MONIVONG: (*with reluctance, but finally feeling obliged to answer*) Excellency, I am indeed apprehensive. It will be a troubled future. The Khmer Rouge in the jungle will feel encouraged to abandon their hitherto low profile. On the other side, our Cambodian military are restless. They want a new US alliance. In the middle, our businessmen are suffering. Our political élites are wondering whether the Kingdom has not been led astray, our traditional neutrality compromised.

(*Lowers his voice.*) I cannot conceal how deeply unhappy I am with where the King has led us.

ROBERT CAMPBELL: Will you resign as Prime Minister, Your Highness? Of course, I hope you do not.

PRINCE MONIVONG: I shall wait upon events.

Int. The King's Official Palace, the Audience Chamber, late afternoon.

THE KING *is receiving* CAMPBELL, *unusually, in the Audience Chamber at his Official Palace: a large, gilded, structure, open to the winds, on a prominence by the Mekong river. Chamberlains in white jackets and baggy 'Sampots' (traditional Court breeches) hover in the background. In the adjacent Throne Room, a large traditional Cambodian 'Pin Peat' orchestra is rehearsing – gongs, xylophones, drums, lutes, cymbals, wind instruments. But the sound is background only, and does not obtrude.*

THE KING, closely observed, is in his mid forties, short, chubby, wearing exquisite clothes from his Italian tailor. Pampered and given to soft living. Smooth skin, colour of dark brown honey, like all upper-crust Khmers. Round eyes, but with slight Mongolian fold. Close-cropped black hair. Exquisitely manicured. Obviously, attentive to his appearance. Nevertheless, a figure charged with energy and possessing a great presence. His moods keep shifting, sometimes solemn, sometimes flippant; sometimes pompously grand, sometimes relaxed and informal. But always linked by a common thread. On this occasion, he chooses to speak English – and speaks it well.

THE KING: We think the language of Shakespeare, this afternoon, if you please, M. le Chargé d'Affaires? (CAMPBELL *bows in his chair*). Once again, you approach Our Throne; and We think We know why. It is not about the peace conference, but about something else, *n'est-ce pas?*

ROBERT CAMPBELL: (*not to be drawn*) Your Majesty, I am truly saddened by the conference débacle. The British Government desire nothing more than the guaranteed independence, neutrality and territorial integrity of your Kingdom.

THE KING: That may be true of the British. But the Americans? It is they who bombard our villages, pursue a hopeless war in Vietnam. But the Americans will go, sooner rather than later. When they have gone, this Kingdom will still be where it is, in Indo-China. We Cambodians have no choice but to learn to live with our neighbours, stand on our own feet – and look to our Chinese friends, in time of need.

ROBERT CAMPBELL: I understand Your Majesty, as to Vietnam. But as to China, now, with the 'Cultural Revolution'?

THE KING: M. le Chargé d'Affaires, China will be always be Cambodia's 'Friend Number One'. By definition. By default.

ROBERT CAMPBELL: Your Majesty has always been a world leader, an inspirational Monarch, a royal activist, in defence of his people. What might the world now expect of Your Majesty?

THE KING: We are sorry to disappoint you, M. Campbell. Sorry to disappoint the wider world, also. But We, the King, shall simply do nothing, nothing at all. The ball is now in the court of the Great Powers. There will be no further initiatives from Phnom Penh. We pray that the Tevodas will continue to protect the Kingdom, as they always have.

ROBERT CAMPBELL: Nevertheless, the people are restless, anxious – and Your Majesty is their much loved Leader.

THE KING: For the present, *le Roi s'amusera*. We have a talent for movie making, as you will be aware – you attended the première of Our last. Perhaps We could persuade M. le Chargé d'Affaires to take part in Our next? We need a handsome, young foreigner, to dance with some of Our Cambodian princesses. To be a 'Number One Twister'. (*Giggles*).

ROBERT CAMPBELL: (*bows politely again*) Should Your Majesty deign to notice me in this manner, then I should naturally be profoundly honoured. But I have already taught your favourite daughter all I know.

THE KING: And you are now teaching Général Lefèvre's daughter …… all you know! She is a beautiful lady – of high blood on her late mother's side. (CAMPBELL, *embarrassed, remains silent*). Ah, what it is to be young. And so *active! (Pauses, for effect; then says, casually)*. You have been seeing Our Commander in Chief and Our Prime Minister, we are further informed? Also Our French Special Advisor?

ROBERT CAMPBELL: (*cautious, but not entirely surprised that the King knows what he has been doing*) I have no secrets from Your Majesty, either in love or diplomacy.

THE KING: We recommend that you stick to love, M. le Chargé d'Affaires. But be of good courage. All shall be well. As for Ourselves, We shall now pay a visit to Paris. To see Our old friend, President de Gaulle, naturally. But also for a week or so's cure at Our usual Spa. Phnom Penh, recently, has been a little …… *mouvementé*. 'Hectic', I think you British would say?

ROBERT CAMPBELL: Allow me to wish Your Majesty a safe journey, an agreeable sojourn in *La Belle France*, and an early return to your Kingdom. There is the Scottish saying: "Haste ye back!".

THE KING: If only *American* diplomats were so charming, so civilised. We, for Our part, wish you every happiness, M. le Chargé d'Affaires in your …… private life.

Ext. The Smart nightclub in Phnom Penh, a few days later.

CAMPBELL *and* MARTINE *have wandered away from their group of companions – who tactfully look the other way.*

> MARTINE LEFEVRE: Bob, I've just heard something. Maurice LeBrun has gone AWOL. The King wanted him, for the Paris trip. Had to fly off without him. Officially, no one knows where he is. But ......
>
> ROBERT CAMPBELL: (*slightly tipsy*) Probably done a runner to Beijing.
>
> MARTINE LEFEVRE: I'm not getting the full picture. But Daddy seems to know something. LeBrun may have been *murdered*. There is ...... evidence that something ...... happened. Signs of a struggle, traces of blood.
>
> ROBERT CAMPBELL: Perhaps he just cut himself shaving – or getting rid of that ridiculous moustache.
>
> MARTINE LEFEVRE: But could it be something to do with his knowing Saloth Sar? Being in touch with the King's enemies? With Lon Nol's "enemy number one"?
>
> ROBERT CAMPBELL: In touch with Pol Pot? But so were *we*, sweetie! (MARTINE *begins to sob*). Sorry. Stupid of me. (*He puts his arm round her shoulder till she recovers*).
>
> MARTINE LEFEVRE: Bob, I'm trying not to lose it. But I'm really scared......

Interlude. Scenes without words.

Troop movements in the city. Armoured cars at major road

junctions. A military cordon around the Royal Palace.

Int. British Embassy Chancery, Campbell's office, mid-morning.

CAMPBELL *and his staff at a crisis meeting.*

ROBERT CAMPBELL: There's been a *coup d'état*, right? What do we know? Colonel?

MILITARY ATTACHÉ: Road blocks everywhere. Royal Palace guarded by tanks.

ROBERT CAMPBELL: But the King's not there. He's on an official visit to Paris.

MILITARY ATTACHÉ: Nevertheless, all the Royal Residences are in army hands. So are all the main government buildings. Significant military movement is reported, around the country. Air Force grounded. Police making themselves scarce, for the time being.

ROBERT CAMPBELL'S PA: Phnom Penh French language radio have already announced a new government, presided over by General Lon Nol, with the Prime Minister as his deputy. According to our local staff, the Cambodian language newscast, just now, quotes Lon Nol as saying that the King is a traitor, to be put on trial, if he returns.

ROBERT CAMPBELL: So the King is, effectively, now in exile? What about foreigners in the capital?

VICE-CONSUL: No report of any trouble, among our own community. I'm due at the Ministry myself, in half an hour.

ROBERT CAMPBELL: I'll do a quick report to London. Then we'd better scatter and get ourselves fully up with the game. Let's meet again, here, at 4pm ....

Interlude. The next four days. Scenes without words.

Vietnamese expatriates in the capital are being rounded up in army lorries, placed in barbed-wire enclosures. Up-country, confused military activity; firing, in some of the villages. Corpses of murdered Vietnamese civilians begin to float down the Mekong river, past Phnom Penh.

Int. British Embassy Chancery, Campbell's office, one month later.

Office meeting, as before.

MILITARY ATTACHÉ: As you know, Bob, Lon Nol announced a major offensive by the Cambodian army two weeks ago. Directed at Vietcong hideouts in the frontier areas. Also a drive against the Khmer Rouge, in the jungle to the North. Initial reports suggest only mixed results. May I go up and take a look see? General Lefèvre is already there, at Lon Nol's field headquarters.

ROBERT CAMPBELL: I suppose you'd better, Colonel. Of course, we don't want to take sides. But London have now recognised Lon Nol's Government. More than that, a new British Ambassador, yes *Ambassador*, is to take post in Phnom Penh. Probably as soon as next month. Can't tell you exactly who, for the moment – but the name has been submitted, in confidence, for

Cambodian *agrément.*

VICE-CONSUL: That's pushing things, Bob, isn't it? Shouldn't HMG be sitting on the fence, for a bit?

ROBERT CAMPBELL: I'm a bit surprised, myself, frankly. But we have to be realistic. The King now seems to be in permanent exile in Beijing.

MILITARY ATTACHÉ: What will happen to *you*, after the new Ambassador's arrived?

ROBERT CAMPBELL: Not a sausage from London so far. Continuity will be important. But, once the new bloke is properly in the saddle, they'll replace me by someone else. No new Ambassador will want me all the time at his elbow, telling him what to do.

Int. The British Ambassador's Residence, one month later.

The new Ambassador, SIR RONALD PEMBRIDGE, *has just arrived in Phnom Penh and taken over.* NOEL RANKIN, *the Australian Ambassador, has come to pay an introductory call. Campbell is present.*

NOEL RANKIN: I wish you every success, Sir Ronald. You will be in good hands with young Campbell here. He's done a terrific job, in the period since your predecessor left. (SIR RONALD *nods politely*). As far as I and my team are concerned, the Australian Embassy is fully at your disposal. Help in any way we can.

Sadly, for me personally, though, it's 'Hail and farewell'. I'm due to give the Foreign Minister my Letters of Recall, tomorrow. The Australian Government are posting me to Cairo – my last overseas post, before retirement at 65.

SIR RONALD: I'm sure we shall all miss you terribly. You have been *en poste* for longer than almost any other current Head of Mission in Cambodia – isn't that right, Bob?

ROBERT CAMPBELL: That's right, Sir.

SIR RONALD: Naturally, you'll be sorry to be going.

NOEL RANKIN: No. Not really. I've seen the best of it. I deplore the *coup d'état*. General Lon Nol's a racist and a cretin. Don't think he stands a snowball's chance in Hell, of survival.

SIR RONALD: (*sceptical*) Really?

NOEL RANKIN: More than just micro-cephalic, Lon Nol's a madman. A superstitious bastard, too. Wears a Buddhist charm around his neck. Thinks it will protect him from all evil. Even bullets from a Chi-Com 'burp' gun.

SIR RONALD: Quite a lot of Cambodian soldiers must be like that, surely?

NOEL RANKIN: Possibly. But the fact is that his military offensives against the Vietcong and the Khmer Rouge have petered out. Yet, despite that, he's even launched limited hot pursuit operations into Vietnam. Unbelievable. Quite unbelievable.

ROBERT CAMPBELL: (*to* SIR RONALD) I'm afraid, Sir, that I hold much the same opinion. You will judge for yourself, when you present your Credentials to General Lon Nol next week.

SIR RONALD: Well, I'll have to see, won't I? At least the Americans seem to like Lon Nol. London, of course, are less gung ho. But we *did* know in advance that the man was going to boot the King out.

Long pause. The Australian and Campbell look stunned. Exchange glances.

NOEL RANKIN: Excuse me? Did I get that right? You heard *in advance*, about the coup? From the Americans, I suppose?

SIR RONALD: Something like that.

ROBERT CAMPBELL: We knew, and we did nothing to discourage it ...... nothing to support the King?

SIR RONALD: Perhaps I've already said too much. However that may be, we have to deal with things as they are, isn't that right, Bob?

CAMPBELL *does not answer, sees* RANKIN *out into his limousine, returns to his Ambassador.*

ROBERT CAMPBELL: I heard what you said, Sir. I won't ask you to repeat it. I will tell no one. But ......

SIR RONALD: Out with it, Bob. What's the problem?

ROBERT CAMPBELL: I'm most awfully sorry, Sir, but I really want no part in this. Frankly, it stinks. Worse than that, it's pure lunacy. (SIR RONALD *raises his eyebrows*). I feel I have no choice but to resign my Commission in the Service. Perhaps you would convey this to Personnel Department in London? Reassure them that – as I believe is customary in these circumstances – I shall go quietly; be totally discreet about my reasons.

SIR RONALD *looks astonished; takes* CAMPBELL*'s arm, walks him about the drawing room, talking earnestly.* CAMPBELL *shakes his head.*

Int. General Lefè vreš villa, the garden, the following day.

CAMPBELL *and* MARTINE *alone. Conversation in English.*

MARTINE LEFEVRE: Daddy says it's going really badly, at the front.

ROBERT CAMPBELL: Where is the General, at the moment? I have a very important request to make of him.

MARTINE LEFEVRE: Back in Paris, for consultations.

ROBERT CAMPBELL: What do you think, darling, about what's going to happen next in this country? Are you planning to leave? Like Devi Sri and her husband? They're in Paris, now, I hear.

MARTINE LEFEVRE: No. This is my country. I'm staying put. Saloth Sar – Pol Pot, as we must now call him – he's the Lon Nol of the Left, I know. But he's a true Cambodian. Mao or no. If he comes out on top, it won't be the end of the world, surely?

ROBERT CAMPBELL: Well, I wouldn't bet on it. He's a monster. Anyway, I am leaving. I've just offered my resignation to the Foreign Office.

MARTINE LEFEVRE: (*taken by surprise, in the grip of conflicting of emotions*) Bob, you can't. The 'Diplomatic' is your life.

ROBERT CAMPBELL: To Hell with that. I'm off. Come with me. I'm going to ask the General for your hand in *marriage*.

MARTINE LEFEVRE: Bob, don't ……

ROBERT CAMPBELL: (*persisting, desperately*) If you don't want London life, we can go to Australia together. I'll become a 'Pommie' merchant banker, in Sydney. You can get a job there, too, with the media. We can make a new life for ourselves. You simply can't stay here. Nor can I. I'm not a

Cambodian. What would I do? Besides, it's not safe.

MARTINE LEFEVRE: I'm sorry, Bob. I love you. But I can't. Can't leave, I mean. This is my country. This is where my roots are. (CAMPBELL *blenches. She has confirmed what he had been beginning to suspect*).

Int. British Embassy Chancery, the Ambassador's Office, the next day.

CAMPBELL *is still in a state of shock, but has slept on things.*

ROBERT CAMPBELL: You wanted to see me?

SIR RONALD: Yes. It's about your resignation, Bob. Have you had any further thoughts?

ROBERT CAMPBELL: I don't know what to think, right now. My private life seems to be in a complete mess. Career-wise, I'm really not sure which way to turn.

SIR RONALD: Well, the FO simply won't hear of you leaving us. Quite out of the question. You've nothing to be ashamed of. Nor have H.M.G. These things happen, for governments and individuals alike. Moments of difficulty; personal stress, too. We all meet it, sooner or later. You've held the fort magnificently. The Secretary of State and all the top brass think the world of you. There's talk of a 'gong'.

ROBERT CAMPBELL: Thank you, Sir …… But what now? I really don't think that I can stay much longer in Phnom Penh. Been here too long, in fact. Perhaps I've gone a bit native?

SIR RONALD: I don't think so. Nor do they. Which brings me to my next question. Will you accept transfer to the Paris Embassy? On promotion to First Counsellor? In charge of the political section there? That's what they're offering you.

ROBERT CAMPBELL: Why Paris, Sir?

SIR RONALD: Something to do with the PM's decision to try again to get into the EEC. Get round the Gaullist veto. Bright new team forming up. People who get on with the French. But to Hell with all that. It's a compliment to you, big time. The PUS says it's the gateway to stardom.

ROBERT CAMPBELL: May I think about it, Sir? Just for 24 hours.

SIR RONALD: Not any longer than that, I'm afraid. The FO want an immediate answer.

Ext. Outside the city, beside a lake, that evening.

CAMPBELL *and* MARTINE *are sitting in his open-top white sports car, looking at a Buddhist temple standing on stilts in the middle of a lake, its golden roof reflected on the surface of the water, in the setting sun. Conversation in English.*

ROBERT CAMPBELL: (*in deadly earnest*) I love you. Martine, I mean it. Come with me to Paris.

MARTINE LEFEVRE: You keep saying that. In your heart though, you know that I can't. I don't *want* to lose you. But let me explain something.

ROBERT CAMPBELL: What is there to explain, dearest? We can all explain. Argue for and against. See both sides of things. But this is our moment. Let's grasp it. It's our destiny. It *has* to be.

MARTINE LEFEVRE: (*speaks slowly, clearly, deliberately, in words which she has evidently been rehearsing in her mind, for some time*) Bob, I have changed. Discovered who I really am. I'm a Khmer, not a French girl. Not a European. Not even the usual upper-class *métisse*. Your Rudyard Kipling was right: East is East and West is West. One has to choose.

As I now see it, foreigners have never been good for us, in my country. Take the French, with their Protectorate. French culture and civilisation rammed down our throats; our own culture and civilisation largely dismissed, apart from French archaeological fascination with Angkor Wat.

Then, Independence. First, vaguely under the US wing. Later, we escaped from that and attempted to square the circle with China and Vietnam. But still as a 'creature country', doing what others wanted – what they thought was best for them. And along came you British and your Peace Conference. Sorry to say it, Bob. But you're just sidekicks of Uncle Sam. (*Campbell winces*) Just British Foreign Secretaries wanting to be seen on TV, as world statesmen.

And then there's me. Martine. I was born a Buddhist, of course. That's where I come from. That's what I really am. But, when I was a child, I was made a Catholic by Daddy. Even now, I'm paraded in the Cathedral for Mass, every Sunday and Feast Day. The clergy are all French, the congregation mostly Vietnamese and French expats. There are almost no Khmer converts. I simply don't fit there.

Later on, I was packed off, to boarding school in France. Mummy died while I was away. Then, when Daddy was appointed to London, he took me with him, to finish my education. I was thoroughly brain-washed, actually, by the Western World.

ROBERT CAMPBELL: What's wrong with being a citizen of the Western World? All educated people are, these days, more or less. You keep your roots. But you grow into the sky.

MARTINE LEFEVRE: I've simply been trying to be what I am not. It doesn't *feel* right, deep inside. But all that's over now. I'm going to become a Buddhist again. I want no further part in the outside world. I just want to be a Cambodian and nothing else. Whoever runs the place – the King, Lon Nol, Pol Pot, whoever. This is my soil, my blood, my destiny. I shall never leave. (CAMPBELL *grabs her hand, tries to interrupt; she puts her finger on his lips and continues*). I cannot, I simply cannot. Not for anyone. Not for Daddy. Not even for you, Bob. I'm so very sorry. You've been everything, done everything, that a girl could dream of. But no. It hurts me to say it, but you're leaving and I'm staying. We must say goodbye. Probably, for ever. Now. Tonight. Take me home, please.

THE ENDING: FORTY YEARS ON

The night scene in the Scottish castle again, as in the Introduction. The two figures are sitting up in bed. LORD CAMPBELL *(as he has since become) is talking with his American wife. He is reaching the end of a long story, telling her everything about his activities in Cambodia, forty years before, and what they meant to him.* LADY CAMPBELL *is a sane, intelligent woman, of normally cheerful disposition. She has been listening intently.*

LORD CAMPBELL: That's the full story, my love. Should have told you all the ins and outs of it a long time ago. Naturally, I followed things from afar, while in Paris. Lon Nol defeated and going into exile. The victory of Pol Pot. Then came a complete news blackout. No one knew what was happening. Despite that, I half expected Martine to turn up, one day, on my doorstep. But while others had fled Phnom Penh, before the Khmer Rouge marched in, she apparently stayed on there. Naturally, I kept in touch with her father, the General, poor man. He, too, had no news. Eventually, we both concluded that she was dead. Murdered in the 'Killing Fields'.

LADY CAMPBELL: Darling, I think I've sensed all this – all that I didn't know, already. Perfectly natural that you knew women before me – loved them, even. But all that is past. You can forget about her.

LORD CAMPBELL: But it's not just a matter of the girl, all those years ago. It's the big picture. The genocide. It's taken years for the truth to get out. A quarter of the entire population – maybe more – put to death or else worked to death. Anyone with any education, or who spoke a word of a foreign language. Anyone, even, who wore glasses. Anyone I knew, who was still around.

LADY CAMPBELL: Bob, terrible though it was – what you are talking about – it's not unique in the wicked world, surely?

LORD CAMPBELL: Maybe worse things *have* happened elsewhere, since then. Tribal massacres in Africa; religious and ethnic slaughter in the Sudan. Not our affair of course, those.

But what about the two wars in Iraq, another in Afghanistan today? To what purpose? And why do we still go blindly along with Washington, whatever they ask? Why all this "Yes, Sir, No Sir, three bags full Sir"! Are we your allies or are we just hired-hands on Uncle Sam's ranch?

LADY CAMPBELL: We Americans sure have our faults. But we're the best allies the Brits have ever had. If you-all are simply too *deferential* to Washington, you only have yourselves to blame. You don't *have* to grovel. You don't all have to be Tony boring Blair, bless him.

Anyway, you've just made my point, Robert. The whole world is full of trouble. Always has been. It's not just Cambodia.

LORD CAMPBELL: But it's still Cambodia, for me, that rankles.

LADY CAMPBELL: Can't you get it into your thick woolly head that IT'S NOT YOUR FAULT? Nor Harold Wilson's, nor President Johnson's. The responsibility lies with the

Communist monsters. It always does. With Mao, Ho, Pol Pot. No different from Joe Stalin – or Adolf Hitler, for that matter!

LORD CAMPBELL: It's not my fault, what eventually happened there. I know that. But I simply can't get it out of my head. And I still feel culpable, to a degree – indirectly, if not directly.

LADY CAMPBELL: Ok, ok. But we're an item now, you and I. Have been for thirty years. It's been a great time, a tight partnership, for both of us. We've watched our children grow up. You've had a wonderful career – Ambassador to the United Nations and all that. They made you a Lord. You've even found your boyhood Faith again – a respected Elder of the Kirk, no less. Don't torture yourself.

LORD CAMPBELL: I was wondering, though, about the nightmares. How to exorcise them. I think it might just help to go back to Cambodia. Just once. The two of us. (*He hugs her*). To show you the place you've heard me talk about so much, over the years.

LADY CAMPBELL: Why, Bob, yes! I'd love to see Cambodia. And I do think that it might help to lay things to rest, finally.

Interlude. Scenes without words.

LORD CAMPBELL *and* LADY CAMPBELL *as tourists in Cambodia. They visit Angkor Wat, including the Temple where Campbell once met Pol Pot. They even locate the site of the tomb of the Crocodile Princess – only to find it badly damaged in the war and now totally deserted. In Phnom Penh, the 'maison flottante' proves long gone; the Ambassador's Residence, destroyed by Pol Pot. But*

CAMPBELL *finds other locales – the Temple in the lake; the Foreign Correspondent's Club. A dinner is given in their honour, at the new British Embassy. Glasses are raised.*

Int. A bedroom suite in the Hotel Royale, Phnom Penh.

CAMPBELL *and* LADY CAMPBELL *are planning what to do on the following day, their last, before returning to Scotland.*

LORD CAMPBELL: Then there's the Genocide Museum, at Tuol Sleng. Used to be a posh High School. I even gave the prizes there at Speech Day, once. The Pol Pot crowd turned it into a Detention Centre. Suspects were brought in, photographed, interrogated, taken off to the Killing Fields to be clubbed to death. Place was run by a chap called "Deuch". I met him, with Pol Pot.

LADY CAMPBELL: (*shuddering*) Well, I'm not going there, Bob, for sure. But you go, if you must.

LORD CAMPBELL: I think I have to, dearest. There's a massive display of mug shots, apparently. Pictures of everyone who passed through. Men, women and children even.

LADY CAMPBELL: (*nodding consent, but looking at him, penetratingly*) Don't stay long. We'll have lunch together on the terrace, when you get back.

Int. The Tuol Sleng Genocide Museum.

CAMPBELL *walks along the wall of photographs, carefully*

examining each one. Sees the faces of Cambodians he once knew – the Prime Minister, Foreign Minister, senior officials, even Hong the driver and three Cambodian former office staff at the Embassy. But he does not find Martine Lefèvre.

Int. A bedroom suite in the Hotel Royale, Phnom Penh.

LADY CAMPBELL *is flicking through a glossy magazine. Looks at her watch. Goes to the window and looks out. Returns to her reading.*

Ext. The Courtyard outside the Museum

CAMPBELL *emerges from the Museum, in search of a taxi to take him back to the hotel. But first, he walks around the buildings, which he recognises from when they were a High School. To one side, near an adjacent Buddhist Monastery, a bare-foot, white-robed figure is pacing slowly to and fro along a path, saying Buddhist prayers.* CAMPBELL *watches, fascinated. Something is familiar to him. Turning back along the path, the figure faces him. A woman, a Buddhist nun. The face marked by the suffering of starvation and forced labour; but wearing a detached expression, like the Buddha.* CAMPBELL *recognises her. Unquestionably,* MARTINE LEFÈVRE*! He experiences a violent upsurge of long repressed emotions – a vivid recall of the past, as if it were yesterday. He runs towards her, stands beside her, holding out his arms.*

LORD CAMPBELL: Martine? Martine?? It's *you*! I've come back. It's *Bob*!

MARTINE *stops. Turns. Stares. After a pause, she recognises* CAMPBELL, *smiles gently, but does not speak, nor hold out her hand. Then she slowly turns back, resumes her path, chanting quietly, losing herself once more in her meditations, content with her destiny. And leaving* CAMPBELL *behind. He backs off, choked. Stumbles out of the courtyard, onto the sidewalk, watched incuriously by the two amputee beggars at the gate. (Ten million unexploded landmines were left lying around, after the last of the hostilities were over).* CAMPBELL *fumbles at the door of a waiting taxi, scrambles clumsily inside, and makes off. Inside the Tuol Sleng complex, the nun continues her pacing, chanting quietly as she goes, at peace with her soul, in pursuit of Enlightenment.*

Int. The bedroom suite at the Hotel Royale, as before.

LADY CAMPBELL: Bob, you look absolutely washed out. Almost as if you'd seen a ghost! I'm so thankful I didn't take in Tuol Sleng with you.

LORD CAMPBELL: It was ghastly. Rudyard was right. East is East. 'Never go back', people say.

LADY CAMPBELL: Darling, thank you for everything, but now we're going home. Remember the movie? "Tomorrow is another day."?

LORD CAMPBELL: I think I'll make a start with the packing, sweetie, if you don't mind. It will give me something to do. So much for the Number One Twister, The Playboy Chargé d'Affaires!

LADY CAMPBELL: Amen to that.

THE END

BACKGROUND READING

The King

The best scholarly biography of Norodom Sihanouk is

>Osborne, Milton, *Sihanouk, Prince of Light, Prince of Darkness*, 1994.

See also, in English, edited and translated by Ambassador Julio A. Andres

>*Shadow over Angkor, Vol. One, Memoirs of H.M. King Norodom Sihanouk*, 2005.

The King's own three-part biography, starting with *Chroniques de guerre ......et d'espoir* and *Souvenirs doux et amers,* concludes with the riveting

>Sihanouk, Norodom, *Prisonnier des Khmers Rouges*, 1986.

The commentaries of two of Sihanouk's former foreign advisers are to be found in

>Zasloff, Joseph J. and Goodman, Allen E. (editors), *Indo-China in Conflict: A Political Assessment*, 1972, Chapter 4: 'The Decline of Prince Sihanouk's Regime' by Donald Lancaster.
>Meyer, Charles, *Derrière le Sourire Khmer*, 1971.

The Cambodian Tragedy

The broadest sweep is to be found in

>Chandler, David P., *The Tragedy of Cambodian History: Politics, War and Revolution since 1945*, 1991.
>Osborne, Milton, *Before Kampuchea*, 1979.

On the Pol Pot pogrom, readers will have seen Haing Ngor's Oscar-winning performance in *The Killing Fields*; but should also read his book

>Ngor, Haing S. with Warner, Roger, *Surviving the Killing Fields*, 1988.

On Pol Pot himself, we now have the authoritative

>Short, Philip, *Pol Pot, The History of a Nightmare*, 2004.

And also the spine-chilling

>Dunlop, Nic, *The Lost Executioner: A Story of the Khmer Rouge*, 2005.
>Affonço, Denise, *To the End of Hell, One Woman's Struggle to Survive Cambodia's Khmer Rouge*, 2005.
>Bizot, François, *The Gate*, 2004.
>Swain, John, *River of Time*, 1998

Plus the well-observed novel

>Burch Donald, Elsie, *A Model American*, 2007.

To which should be added, as essential reading, two magnificent philippics

>Shawcross, William, *The Quality of Mercy: Cambodia, Holocaust and Modern Conscience*, 1984.
>Shawcross, William, *Sideshow: Kissinger, Nixon and the Destruction of Cambodia*, 1979.

Which, in turn, point to the relevant passages, *passim*, in

>Kissinger, Henry, *Diplomacy*, 1994.

A French perspective is furnished by

>Ponchaud, François, *Cambodia, Year Zero*, 1978.

Cambodian Culture

On traditional ballet, the authority is

> Heywood, Denise, *Cambodian Dancers: Celebration of the Gods*, 2008.

I also commend

> Osborne, Milton, *Phnom Penh: A Cultural and Literary History*, 2007.

British Diplomacy

On the original Geneva accords of 1954, there are useful insights, *passim*, from one of the principal architects

> Eden, Anthony, *Full Circle*, 1960.

See also two important sets of documents published by the British Government. First on the Co-Chairmanship of the Geneva Conference generally; second, on Cambodia

> Documents Relating to British Involvement in the Indo-China Conflict 1945-1965, Cmnd. 2834, 1965.
> Recent Diplomatic Exchanges Concerning the Proposal for an International Conference on the Neutrality and Territorial Integrity of Cambodia, Cmnd. 2678, 1965.

For important insights into the British political process and UK foreign policy, at the top

> Hurd, Douglas (Lord Hurd of Westwell), *Choose Your Weapons*, 2010
> Patten, Christopher (Lord Patten of Barnes), *Not Quite the Diplomat*, 2005
> Howe, Geoffrey (Lord Howe of Aberavon), *Conflict of Loyalty*, 1998

Lords Carrington, Howe, Hurd and Owen and Sir Malcom Rifkind, *British Diplomacy: Foreign Secretaries Reflect*, 2007

And, from two professional, career diplomats

Meyer, Christopher, *Getting Our Way*, 2009
Hannay, David (Lord Hannay of Chiswick), *New World Disorder*, 2008

Plus, on the Anglo-US 'Special Relationship'

Meyer, Christopher *DC Confidential*, 2005
Patten, Christopher, *Cousins and Strangers,* 2005

The Cambodian political background to the earlier part of the screen play is set out in

Fielding, Leslie, *Before the Killing Fields: Witness to Cambodia and the Vietnam War*, 2008

HISTORICAL NOTE: SIRIK MATAK'S LAST STAND

Like the fictional Martine Lefèvre, numbers of well-connected but patriotic Cambodians opted to stay on, and accept the consequences, under Pol Pot. Most of them were either put to death, or died from ill-treatment. Among them were Prince Norodom Kanthol, the former Prime Minister, and Prince Sirik Matak, the Head of State's cousin. Both were executed almost at once.

The coup against Norodom Sihanouk in 1970, through the agency of General Lon Nol, was largely instigated by Prince Sirik Matak. Sadly, the Prince and the General had staked everything on the full military support of the US, whereas their ally's overriding preoccupation was not to be drawn further into the Indo-Chinese quagmire. There was no question for the White House of US ground forces being committed in the ensuing battle in Cambodia (which, at least for Henry Kissinger, was merely a 'Sideshow'). Such was the error of the coup that Sirik Matak had set in motion. While a broken General Lon Nol accepted evacuation to Hawaii, his proud and dignified partner chose to stay behind in Phnom Penh. The following is the letter which Prince Sirik Matak addressed to US Ambassador John Dean, before the American Embassy closed on 12 April 1975, and the Ambassador himself, the last to leave, departed by helicopter. After emerging from a few days' sanctuary in the French Embassy compound, the Prince then promptly disappeared from history. It is hard not to admire his personal courage and patriotism, if not his political acumen.

"Dear Excellency and Friend,
    I thank you very sincerely for your letter and for your offer to transport me towards freedom. I cannot, alas, leave in such a cowardly fashion.
    As for you and in particular your great country, I never believed for a moment that you would have this sentiment of abandoning a people which has chosen liberty. You have refused us your protection and we can do nothing about it. You leave and it is my wish that you and your country will find happiness under the sky.
    But mark it well that, if I shall die here on the spot and in my country that I love, it is too bad because we are all born and must die one day. I have only committed this mistake of believing in you, the Americans.
    Please accept, Excellency, my dear friend, my faithful and friendly sentiments.
Sirik Matak"

Also by Leslie Fielding

BEFORE THE KILLING FIELDS: WITNESS TO CAMBODIA AND THE VIETNAM WAR (2008)

A wonderfully entertaining read and hugely germane to many of our present preoccupations in international relations.
Christopher Patten

A vivid picture of the life of a diplomat abroad; usually arduous, sometimes uncomfortable and dangerous; pompous routine varied by passages of the comical and wildly unexpected.
Philip Zeigler

Matches that other outstanding account of duty done on a far frontier – John Master's 'Bugles and Tiger'.
Milton Osborne

Leslie Fielding was one of Britain's more unorthodox and original diplomats… For all students of diplomacy and of Cambodia, this book provides a vivid and colourful picture of life at the sharp end.
International Affairs

Written with panache and verve… a joy to read… reminds us of a seemingly lost world of good fun but also serious thought and action.
Asian Affairs

Fielding gives a gripping account of Cambodia under the mercurial Sihanouk, as the shadows closed in.
Literary Review

Fielding… cuts a dash in the drawing rooms and opium dens of Phnom Penh… As 'Number One Twister', he developed a better relationship with Sihanouk than his US counterparts… He is proud of a time when Britain stood up to America and did not go to war.
Daily Telegraph

KINDLY CALL ME GOD: THE MISADVENTURES OF 'FIELDING OF THE FO', EUROCRAT EXTRAORDINAIRE AND VICE-CHANCELLOR SEMIPOTENTIARY (2009)

This is an entertaining and instructive book, which will give particular pleasure to those of us who have watched with sadness the decline of the Foreign Office as a force in our political life. There are signs now that a Conservative Government would correct the balance and return the FCO to its proper place in forming and directing British foreign policy. Leslie Fielding's book is based on hard reality flowing from practical experience and I strongly recommend it.
Lord Hurd of Westwell

As the reader is taken on a fast canter round the distinguished career course, there are many laughs and no yawns ... We hear the voice of a serious scholar and public servant and cease to be surprised at his success in the world he so engagingly mocks.
Country Life, July 15, 2009

Fantastic! Great reading. Hugely entertaining.
Sir Christopher Ondaatje

I read it with great enjoyment and much admire the wry, irreverent tone.
Tony Howard

How much I enjoyed 'KCMG', both as a roller coaster of adventures/experiences and as a record of diplomatic skills. The final chapters on the role and future of the Foreign Service should be compulsory reading for our political masters, and many others.
John Harding, author of
Road to Nowhere, A South Arabian Odyssey, 1960-1965.

The brilliantly titled 'KCMG' brings together the wide range of cultures encountered by the author and chronicled with consummate panache. Each chapter is crafted like a classic short story and the prose is bursting with energy and sharp observation.
Professor Howard B. Clarke